NOTES ON THE REVOLT

IN THE

NORTH-WESTERN PROVINCES OF INDIA.

NOTES ON THE REVOLT

IN THE

NORTH-WESTERN PROVINCES OF INDIA.

BY

CHARLES RAIKES

JUDGE OF THE SUDDER COURT AT AGRA:

LATE CIVIL COMMISSIONER WITH SIR COLIN CAMPBELL:

AUTHOR OF "NOTES ON THE NORTH-WESTERN PROVINCES OF INDIA."

LONDON

LONGMAN, BROWN, GREEN, LONGMANS, & ROBERTS.

1858

PREFACE.

THE Author of the following Notes has only very recently returned from India. He has observed the anxiety on the part of the educated portion of his countrymen to acquire authentic information as to the present feelings and past conduct of the people of India; and has thought it right to place before the public an account, however hurried and imperfect, of his observations during the past year.

Having no personal adventures to recount, the writer's apology for relating his own history is his desire to support the opinions advanced in the concluding chapters of this book. For it is only from a recital of facts that we can gather material for our future conduct; and in these days any honest narrator of the Indian history of his day may hope for the indulgence of the public.

London : July, 1858.

CONTENTS.

CONTENTS.

NOTES ON THE REVOLT

&c.

CHAPTER I.

THE FIRST OUTBREAK.

On the morning of the 11th May, 1857, I was seated in my library at Agra, quietly preparing for the labour of the day, when a slip of paper was placed on my table. I read as follows:—

"*The Mofussilite Extra.*

"Agra, Monday, May 11, 1857.

"A telegraphic message from Meerut* states that the troopers of the 3rd Cavalry have mutinied, setting fire to their own lines and several officers' bungalows, killing and wounding all European

---

* Meerut is 131 miles north-west from Agra. There is a good cross road from Agra to Allygurh on the Grand Trunk road. The distance from Agra to Allygurh is 51 miles, and from Allygurh to Meerut, 80 miles. This telegraphic message was a private one, sent to some resident of Agra, who was about to start for Meerut, and was thus saved from probable destruction.

officers and soldiers they could find near their lines.

" In a station like Meerut, with the 6th Dragoons, 60th Rifles, and European artillery, it may be presumed that the mutineers had a very short race of it. Further particulars have been sent for.

" The Calcutta Government Gazette announces the disbanding of seven companies of the 34th Native Infantry.

" Letters from Meerut state that the eighty-five troopers 3rd Cavalry have been tried. Those most to blame have been sentenced to ten years' imprisonment, others to five years.

I felt, as may be supposed, the gravity of the event thus suddenly announced. It was the bursting of the thunder-cloud I had been long and anxiously watching; or rather, the mine so long charged had at last been sprung. The fabric of the Bengal army was tottering to ruin; to pull down with it the civil and political institutions which that army had for a hundred years supported.

At noon the judges of the Sudder Court assembled as usual. Business went on according to rule. Cases were tried, pleadings heard, and decrees passed. But the mind of the European functionaries was, more or less, absent. That thirst for news from the distant scene of action, which became so distressing and lasted so long, had begun.

Mr. Henry Byng Harington, for many years the ornament of our bench, had just resigned his seat. His carriages were packed for a short journey to the hill station of Missouri. His route lay viâ Meerut; and from Missouri he was to have proceeded at once to Calcutta, to take his place as member (for the North-Western provinces) of the Legislative Council of India. His journey was stopped; and I may here remark that, with rare public spirit and self-devotion, he subsequently determined, at the desire of the Lieutenant-Governor, Mr. Colvin, to remain in Agra, though strongly tempted to place himself and his family in comparative security, by proceeding, as in the ordinary course of duty he was bound to do, to join his appointment in Calcutta.*

His advice was often most valuable to us all; and I only express the sentiments of the community of Agra, when recording our obligations to Mr. Harington for sharing our dangers and privations with us.

* The road *down* the country from Agra to Calcutta, viâ Mynpoorie and Cawnpore, was not closed to travellers for some days after the 11th May.

CHAP. II.

BEFORE attempting to describe the immediate effect of the mutiny at Meerut and Delhi on the population of the North-Western provinces, I briefly sketch the state of things existing before the revolt.

The North-Western provinces, so called, are not now our most northern and western possessions in India, but obtained their designation before the Punjab was annexed. Stretching from the sources of the Ganges and Jumna on the north, to the Caramnasa on the south, the territory is parcelled out into six great divisions, comprising in all thirty-one zillahs or districts, with an area of 72,000 square miles, and a population of thirty millions.* Each division takes in five or six districts. At head-quarters (civil) in every division resides the Commissioner, with authority in police and revenue affairs over the district officers, designated " Magistrate and Collector" in each district of the division.

Courts of civil and criminal justice under Zillah Judges are held at the different stations, the juris-

* The reader who may wish for further statistical information is referred to Appendix A, in which the area, population, and revenue of the North-Western provinces are detailed.

diction of the judge extending over one, or some-times two, districts.

The commissioners of revenue and police, the Zillah Judges, and the Collector Magistrate, all belong to the Covenanted Civil Service of the East India Company.

To superintend the working of this system, we had at Agra, when the mutiny broke out, a Lieutenant-Governor, the Sudder Court (Sudder Dewannie and Nizamut Adawlut*), and the Re-venue Board.

Just one year before the mutiny, I was summoned from the Punjab to take my seat as a judge of the Sudder Court. Having been for three years Com-missioner of Lahore, I had opportunities of com-paring the systems of government in the Punjab and North-Western provinces. My prepossession in coming to Agra was in favour of the Punjab plan. I still retain that prepossession. I therefore, in describing the state of the North-Western pro-vinces from May 1856, to May 1857, write without any prejudice in favour of the system of government within that territory, to which system, as will here-after be shown, I entertain strong objections. But I had, as forming a part of the local administration,

* Chief civil and criminal tribunal. Has power of life and death. The judges formerly were the Governor-General and members of council; and now, under Her Majesty's warrant, have precedence in India over other civil officers not governors or members of the Executive or Legislative Councils. Appeals in civil cases of 1000l. and upwards, lie to Her Majesty in Council. In other cases the orders of the court are final.

excellent opportunities of observing the general working of the government and state of the people.

I have already described * the condition of the people in the North-Western provinces at the period of the annexation of the Punjab. Making some little abatement for the youth and zeal of the writer, I still adhere to that description, and on my return to the provinces from Lahore, I found no deterioration in the state of the people. Mr. Colvin, who in 1853 had succeeded Mr. Thomason as Lieutenant· Governor, had worked hard and well; the operations of the police were closely supervised, the Lieutenant-Governor watching the conduct of each Magistrate, I may almost say of every criminal case, with untiring vigilance; numerous proclaimed offenders, who had been at large for the last twenty years, had been apprehended and brought to trial. Murderous affrays were gradually becoming more rare.

It was no fault of Mr. Colvin's that our civil courts were still nearly as unpopular as ever. He had done what he could to reform them, and the tendency of legislation towards simplicity and ra-

* "Notes on the North-Western Provinces of India," published by Chapman and Hall in 1852. In alluding to this book, I would apologise by observing, that most of it was written when I was very young, and consequently in too ambitious a style. Since I wrote it, my feelings towards the people of India may have been changed by late events; but, nevertheless, the principles advocated in the Notes are, I believe, sound. It may be difficult hereafter to love the people of India, but we must nevertheless still cultivate their affections if we would hold the country.

pidity of procedure had been sufficiently marked. A great change * for the better was in contemplation, when the mutiny put a stop to all further progress in the road to civilisation.

In revenue matters I found the Collectors of districts more pressed than ever by the requirements of the government for information, statistics, &c., the fault of the system being, that too much detail of work done was expected. The pressure of the land revenue, as in former years, was generally equal; if not moderate, certainly not excessive. It was a full, but just land tax, firmly enforced, without any frequent resort to measures of distress, and on the whole punctually paid.

So far as the happiness of a nation consists in general peace, order, personal safety and liberty, with abundance of the necessaries of life, the people of the North-Western provinces were happy.

They disliked, for very sufficient reason, our system of civil procedure. The police, chosen from amongst themselves, and superintended by native subordinate magistrates, were unpopular, because every Asiatic man with power in his hands is apt to abuse that power, and at best to think too much of himself and too little of the public. Lastly, our village educational measures were disliked and suspected.

But, for all this, I repeat that the mass of the

* The new Code of Civil Procedure, prepared by Her Majesty's Commissioners in London, was about to be introduced when the mutiny broke out.

people were quiet and as contented as any semi-barbarous people can be with a strong government. Not a whisper of treason, rebellion, or disaffection was heard ; agriculture and commerce were thriving, population increasing, when on this busy working scene broke the revolt.

CHAP. III.

CIRCUMSTANCES prevented me from keeping up my accustomed regular journal, but I shall present to the reader occasional extracts from the short notes recorded, which will enable me to carry on the gloomy narrative of the past year, all reference to my own private sufferings being omitted.

" *Sunday, May* 10*th.* — A quiet day.

" *Monday,* 11*th.* — This Mofussilite Extra* was put into my hands. Harington was to have started for the hills this afternoon; he will pause.

" *Tuesday,* 12*th.* — Bishop Persico (Roman Catholic Bishop of Agra) and one of the French missionaries proceeding to Thibet, spent the evening with us. No regular post in from Allygurh this morning. The Meerut mails stopped by the mutineers.

" *Wednesday,* 13*th.*—Summoned to government house to take part in a council of war."

Here I pause to look back to that scene. Mr. Colvin had received reports from which he was led to suppose, that the mutineers from Meerut, after sacking Delhi and committing atrocities there, were marching on Agra. I found the Lieutenant-

---

* See ante, pages 1 to 2.

Governor already exposed to that rush of alarm, advice, suggestion, expostulation and threat, which went on increasing for nearly two months until he was driven broken-hearted into the fort. The critic may ask, why did Mr. Colvin allow any man to advise, threaten, or expostulate? My answer is, that his position from the first was one of extreme difficulty; he did his duty to the best of his ability, and his devotion to the public good ended only with his life. To say that he made some mistakes is to say that he was a man.

I was surprised to find that the Lieutenant-Governor had already taken into his confidence some of the Mahomedan high officials. Whilst talking, he handed me with a smile, one of the notes pouring in. It was from an able public officer, who had great opportunities of knowing what was going on in the city, and contained a solemn warning to His Honour to beware of the knife of the assassin.

One officer rushed in to suggest that we should all retire to the fort, another to ask what was to be done at the jail, a third to speak about provisions, a fourth about the sepoy regiments in cantonments. Every man was anxious to do his best, but to do it in his own way. It was decided to brigade the troops early next morning in the park surrounding Government House, the Brigadier to command, and the Lieutenant-Governor on his elephant to accompany the brigade, and so we were all to march out to meet the enemy.

After satisfying myself that at least a company

of the European regiment had been ordered into
the fort, professedly to support, but in reality to
over-awe the sepoys who had hitherto formed the
garrison, and after expressing my doubt as to the
fact of any mutineers being near us, I retired with
Mr. Harington, promising to attend the Lieutenant-
Governor in the morning.

"Mr. Thornhill, Secretary to Government, came
with his family to our house to sleep, or rather to
pass the night, for too many reports and notes
came in to allow him much rest. He observed to
me, that the sepoys held our forts, treasuries, and
arsenals all over the country, and that if they rose
at once upon us there was no European force to
put them down. Matters certainly looked bad;
however, the report of the advance of the mutineers upon Agra was contradicted.

"*Thursday*, 14*th*. — The troops were brigaded
this morning, not at Government House, but at
cantonments. The salute fired when Mr. Colvin
came on parade frightened the ladies in the civil
lines, as they supposed a fight between the Europeans and natives had begun. Colvin addressed
the 3rd Europeans first, telling them to feel no
distrust of their native fellow-soldiers, whom they
should consider brothers in arms — (our honest fellows looked as if they would nevertheless like to
have a shot at their brothers). He added, the
rascals at Delhi have killed a clergyman's daughter,
and if you should have to meet them in the field
you will not forget this.

"Then came the sepoys' turn. The Lieutenant-

Governor said, that he fully trusted them, asked them to come forward if they had any complaints to make, and offered to discharge on the spot any man who wished to leave his colours. Prompted by their officers to cheer, the sepoys set up a yell; they looked, however, with a devilish scowl at us all. I rode through the city home, turning back crowds of East Indians and others who were struggling down to the fort. Many who had taken refuge there last night came out. Meerut mail in.

"*Friday,* 15*th.*—A stupid panic last night again; we slept at the Candaharie Bagh.* I patrolled with Muir, Thornhill, Dashwood and Lowe. Better rumours from Delhi, but no dak in thence or from Meerut. Telegraphic communication with Calcutta stopped."

Here I must record the indignation with which on Thursday evening we learned that the mutineers at Meerut, after firing the station, murdering our countrymen, women and children, and breaking the jail, had been permitted to retire quietly on Delhi, taking their barbers, water-carriers, bag and baggage, just as if they had been going an ordinary march. I now know that Major Rosser, of H. M. 6th Carbineers, asked permission to follow them with cavalry and guns. If he had been allowed to do so, it is quite possible, and indeed probable, that

---

* A masonry house belonging to the Rajah of Bhurtpore, and occupied by my colleague, Mr. Morgan, who kindly allowed it to be used as a stronghold for the " Civil Lines."

the mutiny, for the present at least, might have been crushed.

"*Saturday*, 16*th*.—Gwalior Contingent (small detachments of all arms) coming in. Orders from Meerut to throw the European regiment into the fort over-ruled by Mr. Colvin, who has received full power and authority from Lord Canning to act during the crisis as may seem best. Finding that Mr. Colvin wished to raise some Irregulars at Mynpoorie, I volunteered, and got written orders* to proceed and raise a couple of hundred men. But as I was making preparations, it was represented to Mr. Colvin that the departure of a Sudder Judge from Agra just now would add to the general alarm of the natives in the city; so he sent Thornhill to ask me to stay, thanking me handsomely for the offer.

"*Monday*, 18*th*.—Cheering news from Etaweh, of the 9th Native Infantry cutting up some of the

---

* Mr. Raikes is deputed to raise 200 cavalry in the Mynpoorie, Etaweh, Furuckabad, and Etah districts.

Pay. 20 rupees per mensem, certain for two years. Not to be employed beyond the division.

Duty. To protect roads, towns, villages, and poor people from plunder. The officers of all districts with whom Mr. Raikes is in communication to be told that they need not bo under the least apprehension, and should not think of moving their families or property, or making any change whatever in their daily habits. The insurgents will be promptly and effectively put down.

All civil officers will co-operate with Mr. Raikes in carrying out these orders, and the collectors will honour his drafts.

                    (*Signed*)   T. R. COLVIN.
May 16th, 1857.

run-away troopers. At court some alarming letters from ———, who professes to know of some great impending dangers. The Gwalior Contingent men ask if the flour supplied to their camp is from government stores. If so they will not touch it. This is not pleasant, they have got hold of the bone dust story.*

" *Tuesday*, 19*th.*—The news from all sides seems good. Our native allies rallying around us, the European troops hastening down from the hills upon Delhi, and we hear that many Englishmen and women have escaped alive from Delhi.

" *Thursday*, 21*st.*—Heard of the fall of Allygurh to the mutineers. An alarm in the city, and a general rush to the Candaharee Bagh. I rode down and brought some ammunition from the jail to the bagh, in which hundreds of the Christian population had hastily assembled. I then rode to French's school; found French there alone, the other missionary having gone to look after his wife."

I must pause here to record the impression made upon my mind by the calmness and coolness of Mr. French. Every Englishman was handling his sword or revolver. The road covered with carriages, people hastening right and left to the rendezvous at Candaharee Bagh. The city folk

---

* One of the many inventions circulated amongst the sepoys, in order to produce disaffection, was, that the Government had cows' bones made into powder, and mixed with the flour sold in the bazaars, in order to pollute their food, a bone being an abomination in the eyes of the Hindoo.

running as for their lives, and screaming that the mutineers from Allygurh were crossing the bridge. The *"bud-maashes"** twisting their moustachios and putting on their worst looks. Outside the college all alarm, hurry and confusion. Within calmly sate the good missionary, hundreds of young natives at his feet, hanging on the lips which taught them the simple lessons of the Bible. And so it was throughout the revolt. Native functionaries, highly salaried, largely trusted, deserted and joined our enemies, but the students at the government, and still more, the missionary, schools kept steadily to their classes; and when others doubted or fled, they trusted implicitly to their teachers and openly espoused the Christian cause.

I may add my belief that, owing partly to this good disposition of the students, and partly to the zeal of the missionary, Mr. French's missionary college was about the last to close and the first to re-open of all our public institutions at Agra, during the period of the revolt.

"*Friday*, 22*nd*.—Plenty of alarmists. In the morning I was assured that the Principal Sudder Ameen (native judge) was circulating seditious reports. I traced out the story and found it to be without foundation. In the evening ——— came over in the greatest excitement, having heard of

---

* Budmaash means a man of bad livelihood. Our Indian cities unfortunately teem with such characters, ripe for mischief and longing for anarchy.

the fall of Mynpoorie; this turned out to be un-
true.   A fire at night.

"*Saturday*, 23*rd*. — We went to see Lady
Outram, who had been compelled to fly, as for her
life, from Allygurh.   She was suffering much
from her feet, having been obliged to walk without
shoes part of the way from Allygurh.   To-day's
alarm was that the Mahratta horse (part of
Scindia's body guard sent to attend upon the
lieutenant-governor) were to be sent away.   I
was just going at Muir's suggestion to remonstrate
against this move with Colvin, when it was
countermanded.

"*Sunday*, 24*th*.—We had a quiet night, attended
divine service.   Captain Greathed called to ask
for a body of volunteers to escort the Gwalior
guns towards Allygurh.   I was just out on this
business when I heard that the expedition was
countermanded.   Hassan Ali Thanadar (police
superintendent), of Seersagunge (in the Mynpoorie
district), came in.   He says that John Power is
holding his own well at Mynpoorie ; and that Rao
Bowannie Singh has taken the government treasury into his fort.   I gave him letters to several
leading men to encourage them to rally round
Power just now.

"*Monday*, 25*th*. — The Eed festival is over,
and people seem happier : fires at night now and
then.

"*Tuesday*, 26*th*, up to end of the week.—Much
anxiety about Indian affairs.   Regiments mutiny-
ing right and left."

As I copy this journal the reminiscences of the period come full upon me. I pause for a moment to recall the past, and to describe our condition thus far.

As yet, setting panics aside, Agra had been quiet. No blood, either of natives or Europeans, had been shed. Yet, from the 11th May to the end of the month, every day and every night had been full of anxiety. Hitherto we had been the lords of the nations, flattered, courted by the people, caressed by fortune, confident in our own strength. How soon might we, like our Christian brethren and sisters at Delhi, be wanderers, house-less, with a blood-thirsty enemy on our track, or what at first we dreaded as much, shut up, amidst famine and pestilence, in a fort.

Amidst the civilization of the nineteenth century, among libraries, printing presses, colleges, and cathedrals, we found ourselves on the verge of barbarism.

Delhi too, had all these types of a thriving Euro-pean civilization a few days back; now what re-mained at Delhi of western art, but ruins soaked with Christian blood ? The sepoys of the 44th and 67th Regiments of Native Infantry, whose comrades at Delhi were revelling amongst the fragments of our churches and palaces, longed to bring about a like ruin at Agra. Nightly fires and secret meet-ings told us their temper. How soon might we expect them to throw off the mask of subordination, and carry fire and sword into our dwellings ? How long would the Gwalior Contingent army remain

c

staunch, with its infantry, cavalry, and powerful siege artillery? Their temper too had been shown; how many days more would they fawn upon the officers whom they had already marked for destruction? The youthful Scindia, with his passion for arms, and the traditions of the past burning in his breast, what chance was there of his fidelity? Mutiny had already broken out at Allygurh, who could calculate on the troops at Mynpoorie, Furuckabad, and Etaweh? Our own local police, on whom muskets and ball ammunition had been lavished, and who already began to scowl upon the Christian, how far were they to be trusted?

Such were the questions which perplexed the mind of every man capable of comprehending the gravity of the crisis. They who had friends or relations in Oude, Cawnpore, or Rajpootana, were further tormented by daily reports of fresh outbreaks, murders, and mutinies.

The men who cared least for all this were those most in danger, our young officers in the native regiments. They rode, swam, and played at billiards with as much gaiety as though they had not nightly to sleep in the lines amongst a set of ruffians thirsting for their blood. My own position and that of my colleagues was not an enviable one. With superior opportunities of knowing the extent of the dangers which overhung not only our wives, sisters, and children, but our empire in India; we were obliged daily to take our seat on the bench, and listen to long arguments about debts and mortgages, which we suspected would soon be cleared off by the intervention of anarchy rather than law. We had to grant injunctions which nobody attended to, and to pass decrees which no man could execute. And specially irksome was this mockery to one like me, who had near and dear relations at a distant station exposed to the full fury of the mutiny.   At the same time the Sudder Court had no executive power, and was helpless, or nearly so, either for good or evil.

Amidst all these various causes for anxiety, the most immediate to the Christian community of Agra, was the hourly expectation of a local sepoy revolt.   It was therefore a positive relief to me when, on the night of the 30th June, Messrs. Muir and Farquhar called, and told me that there had been mutiny and murder at Muttra, and that Government had determined to disarm the native regiments at daybreak next morning.

CHAP. IV.

SIR HENRY LAWRENCE AND HIS OLD STAFF.

I HAVE said that the detachments from the native infantry regiments, stationed at Muttra, mutinied on the night of Saturday the 30th. On the same night, at the same hour, the sepoys in the distant capital of Lucknow rose to a similar work of conflagration, robbery, mutiny, and murder. On the afternoon of Saturday, by the last regular post that for nearly a twelvemonth left Lucknow, Sir Henry Lawrence despatched the following letter to me.

"Lucknow, May 30th.

"My dear Raikes,

"Kindly give me an occasional line until Delhi is taken. We are pretty jolly, but if the commander-in-chief delay much longer he may have to recover Cawnpore, Lucknow, and Allahabad; indeed all down to Calcutta.

"We are in a funny position. While we are intrenching two posts in the city, we are virtually besieging four regiments (in a quiet way) with three hundred Europeans. Not very pleasant diversion to my civil duties. I am daily in the town four miles off for some hours, but reside in cantonments guarded by the gentlemen we are besieging!

"Send a copy of this to my brother George at Ajmere; my health is very good *for me*.

"Christian* is doing very well and pluckily.

* Sir Henry here alluded to my son-in-law, George Jackson Christian, Commissioner of Seetapore in Oude, who, with his wife and one child, perished on the 3rd June, in the massacre at that station. The remaining child, a little girl of three years, was rescued at the time by the heroism of Capt. Burnes, son of James and nephew of Sir Alexander and Charles, who, at the risk and, as events turned out, probably at the sacrifice of his own life, carried her off in his arms. She shared the captivity of this noble-hearted man with Miss Jackson and Mrs. Orr, and sunk under her sufferings, in Lucknow, after several months' imprisonment.

Her preserver was put to death, at an earlier period, by the sepoys, thus adding to the list of martyrs which the brave family of Burnes has produced.

On the very day, May 30th, when Sir Henry thus briefly eulogised my son-in-law, George Christian too was writing to me his last letter, in which he thus alluded to the state of affairs.

. . . .

"All quiet here ; and, throughout my division, the people seem well disposed, and the regular regiment here, the 41st, are quite quiet.

"And I have in position 950 men, so that, if things go wrong elsewhere, and they are tempted to rise, we could (D.F.) crush them in an hour.

"Our position here is strong, and our force so *mixed* (an important point now-a-days), that I am prepared to send, if required, reinforcements to the tune of 250 soldiers of the 9th Oude Irregular Infantry in any direction, and still retain enough to thrash the 41st Native Infantry.

"Throughout the province there is quiet, and at every station preparations have been made.   .   .   .   .

What I most fear are risings in the districts and
the Irregulars getting tainted.   Daily I have reports of conspiracies all around.   Show this to Mr.
Colvin and Reid.*

" Yours very sincerely,
" H. LAWRENCE."

Every Englishman will forgive me if I wander
from my subject for a moment, to offer my humble
tribute of affection to the man who, perhaps above
all others, has done honour to the name of English-

" Sir Henry Lawrence has arranged admirably, and come
what will, we are prepared.   .   .   .   .   .   .

" The village system, which makes all men equal in their
poverty, is now fairly on its trial in the disturbed districts, and
government has hardly a single man of influence to look to in
them.   Their army is the same, a dead level; no gentlemen, no
difference save in military rank.

" I love neither system, but I hope our eyes will now be
opened to Robertson's prophecy on the inevitable tendency of
our system."

I have been told by native fugitives from Seetapore, that
when the 41st mutinied George Christian called out his Irregulars, who gradually deserted as the sepoys approached.   Although my son-in-law treated the matter so lightly in this his
last letter, I knew from former letters and from other sources
that he had been warned, not only of the prevailing disaffection
in Oude, but also that, either owing to his name or character,
he had long been marked by the 41st regiment as the first
Englishman to be shot at Seetapore.   Capt. Orr had, to my
knowledge, written to warn him.   However, as Sir Henry
writes, George Christian was, like his brethren in both services, doing "pluckily," and, like too many of them, he and all
that belonged to him perished.

* Reid means E. A. Reade, an old friend of Sir Henry,
member of the Revenue Board at Agra.

man in India. To know Sir Henry was to love
him.

In 1853, when I was on my way to Lahore, and
Sir Henry was leaving the Punjab, I had witnessed the unbounded regard which all classes
displayed to his person. During my term of office
at Lahore, I had occasion, in the discharge of my
public duty, to prosecute and bring to punishment
men who owed their appointments to Sir Henry's
favour. Instead of resentment, he honoured me
with increased regard, acknowledging that I had
exercised a necessary severity. In March, 1857,
at Agra, when on his way to take charge of his
new duties as Chief Commissioner of Oude, I had
much daily and unreserved intercourse with Sir
Henry. I found him, as it were, ripening fast,
alike for that goal of human glory which he was
soon to attain, and for that sublimer change which
so quickly awaited him.

His heart seemed overflowing with Christian
charity. I remember that, in returning a volume
of Memoirs of Bishop Sandford, he wrote to call
my attention to the following passage, which he
had marked with a pencil. " My fears for those
who retain a spirit of unforgiveness are over-
powering: I will sincerely declare to you, that I
could not myself pray to God or ask His pardon
for my many transgressions before I go to bed at
night with any comfort, or with any hope of being
heard, unless I were conscious that I did from my
heart forgive as I ask to be forgiven." (Vol. ii.
pp. 106, 107.) When next I met him, as we walked

to the early church service (it was the time of Lent), he poured out his heart on the beautiful topic of Christian forgiveness, adding, that he had sent a copy of the extract above quoted to a distinguished officer, once his friend, who had taken deep offence at some public act of Sir Henry's. For every child that he met in my own family, in the missionary or other public schools, he had a word of kindness or encouragement. Incidentally he told me that the secret of his ability to support those public institutions with which his name will for ever be associated, was to be found in his abstinence to the utmost from all sorts of personal expense. During his stay in Agra, while his hand was open to every one else, he resolutely avoided spending money on himself.

He went to Oude, not without feelings of ambition, but principally from a high sense of duty, whilst he had the strongest medical opinions of the necessity of an immediate change to Europe, and when suffering, as he told me, "from a dozen different complaints."

At that moment I was preparing a little publication on the Punjab. Sir Henry asked me to visit him at Lucknow in the following September, when he would place all his private papers* connected with his Punjab career at my disposal.

With this same object in view I applied to Colonel Herbert Edwardes, on his journey viâ

---

* Sir Henry's papers had been sent to Bombay, at which port he had proposed to embark when he was stopped by Lord Canning's summons to Lucknow.

Agra to Peshawur, on his return from Lucknow in April, 1857, to give me a memorandum of Sir Henry's old staff in the Punjab previous to annexation.

Colonel Edwardes, as ready with his pen as with his sword, as all the world knows, very kindly noted down for me the following graphic description. The public will thank me for throwing open this little gallery of portraits. One of the originals, John Nicholson, has, alas! gone down already to the hero's grave amidst the tears of his countrymen, under the walls of Delhi.

Sir Henry's " Old Staff" in the Punjab previous to annexation.

ARTHUR COCKS.	EDWARD LAKE.
GEORGE LAWRENCE.	JOHN R. BECHER.
JAMES ABBOTT.	JOHN NICHOLSON.
GEORGE M'GREGOR.	HERBERT EDWARDES.
HARRY LUMSDEN.	REYNELL TAYLER.

ARTHUR COCKS

was the " chief assistant to the resident" when Sir Henry Lawrence was administering the Punjab for the Maharajah. He imbibed all Sir Henry's feelings, and became greatly attached to the chiefs and people. He hardly stayed a year after annexation, and left the Punjab because he could not bear to see the fallen state of the old officials and sirdars. (He had been

unfortunately made Deputy Commissioner of Lahore, where he saw this *only :* had he got a country
district he would have been happy, I believe, in
the real good of the lower orders.) He has carried
Sir Henry's feelings with him to the North Western
Provinces, and acknowledges him as " the good
genius" of his public *creed.*   The Sudder Court of
Agra can best judge if the creed be orthodox.*

George Lawrence

was Sir Henry's elder brother, and formed his own
character.   Best as a soldier.   Held command of
Peshawur during the second Sikh war of 1848-49,
and kept the large Sikh garrison from overt rebellion up to a very late period of the war.

Left the Punjab when it became a purely civil
administration.

Is now officiating agent to the Governor-General
in Rajpootana.

James Abbott,

when assistant-resident, was deputed by Sir Henry
to receive charge of the Huzara frontier from Maharajah Goolab Singh (to whom it had been
originally assigned, but who proved utterly unable
to control it; thus leading to an exchange of

---

* In reply to this allusion, I can only say that the Sudder
Court hold Mr. Arthur Cocks in the very highest esteem; my
own opinion of his noble character and conduct will be given
further on.

territory—Huzara reverting to the Sikhs and they giving up some quiet tracts to the Squeezer!)

James Abbott was instructed to reduce the revenue of Huzara to something nominal as the only way of re-peopling and pacifying the country. He did so; going from valley to valley with his mission of hope; and won the confidence of the tribes.

He remained among them afterwards as coadjutor of the Sikh governor, Sirdar Chuttur Singh, the father-in-law of Maharajah Duleep Singh.   In 1848, the Sirdar headed the Sikh insurrection, and James Abbott found himself placed, like others of Sir Henry's assistants, in the strange position of raising the Mahomedan subjects of the Sikhs against the rebel Sikh chiefs, to preserve if possible the Sikh raj, of which the British government was guardian.

The mountaineers of Huzara could not contend with the Sikh brigades, but they remained faithful to James Abbott, and protected him for many months, till the battle of Goojarat ended the campaign.   Then followed annexation and the introduction of a system of civil administration throughout the Punjab.   James Abbott became Deputy Commissioner of Huzara, and remained so till 1853, when he resigned the charge.   Thus he was six years in Huzara; and he left it amidst the unfeigned regrets of the people.   During his rule, exiles driven out by the Sikhs ten, twenty, thirty, forty years before, had flocked back again from beyond the border, and been resettled on their

paternal lands;—Huzara had passed from a deso-
lation to a smiling prosperity;—it was *he* who had
worked the change—a single Englishman;—he
had literally lived among them as their patriarch—
an out-of-door, under-tree life; every man, woman
and child in the country knew him personally, and
hastened from their occupations to welcome and
salute him as he came their way.

The children especially were his favourites. They
used to go to "Kâkâ Abbott" (Uncle Abbott)
whenever their mouths watered for fruit or sugar-
plums. He never moved out without sweetmeats
in his pocket for the chance children who might
meet him, and as plentiful a supply of money for
the poor. He literally spent all his substance on
the people, and left Huzara, it is believed, with
only his month's pay.

His last act was to invite the country—not the
neighbours—but all Huzara, to a farewell feast on
the Nârâ hill; and there for three days and nights
he might be seen with long grey beard over his
breast, and grey locks far down his shoulders,
walking about among the groups of guests, and
hecatombs of pots and cauldrons—the kind and
courteous host of a whole people.

What is the result?

The district of Huzara, which was notorious for
its long continued struggles with the Sikhs, is now
about the quietest, happiest, and most loyal in the
Punjab.

JOHN BECHER

is James Abbott's successor; and is to Huzara all that Abbott *was.* High praise. His cutcherry is not "from ten till four" by the regulation clock; but all day, and at any hour of the night that anybody chooses; — the "*barahduree*" system of administration—living in a house with twelve doors, and all open to the people.

He was at Buttala before—and did the same there.*

GEORGE MACGREGOR,

now resident at Moorshedabad, was another of Sir Henry's assistants; but he had achieved his own

---

* I had the happiness of being associated with John Becher, who served under me as deputy commissioner of Buttala when I was commissioner of Lahore. When he left Buttala for Huzara, the people followed him in crowds, weeping and invoking blessings on his head. As a sample of "the school of Henry Lawrence," I give an extract from a kind letter which I received from Major Becher on my departure from Lahore for Agra.

. . . .

"Let me also on paper shake you by the hand, and wish 'Good bye' to you and to Mrs. Raikes in the same spirit as the 'Good-bye' at Umritsur, when I first met you, and all were giving an affectionate farewell to their old friend and master, Sir Henry Lawrence.

"Some day I may meet you again, and recall old memories of the Punjab, though I am sure you will never forget the Punjab portion of your life, nor will the Punjab be forgetful of you.

"May much of its *old spirit* remain!

"Huzara, March 28, 1856."

fame, and formed his own style, as political officer
to the garrison of Jellalabad.   [1]

MAJOR HARRY LUMSDEN,

of the Guides, was picked out from his corps by
Sir Henry Lawrence, and has proved the prince of
border soldiers. He raised the Guide Corps; armed
it with rifles; dressed it in mud-colour; and in
endless skirmishes achieved a name with it which
is as well known in Affghanistan as India. It has
since been the model for the Punjab Irregular
Force. He has now been selected to watch the
Persians at Candahar—a high mark of the confidence of government.

EDWARD LAKE

is another of Sir Henry's assistants;—but he was
detached under Sir John Lawrence in the Jalun-
dhur Doab, and must rather be regarded as a disciple
of both brothers, uniting the best points of both
systems. Brave—kind—active—indefatigable—
accessible—thoughtful—chivalrous and wise:—
he was as much at home as a soldier leading on the
Bhawulpoor army at Mooltân— as he is in administering a highly organised system of civil
government. As a leader he lived among his
soldiers; as a civilian he lived among the people.
By both he has been loved and respected. He may
be taken as the best type the Punjab affords of the
military civilian.

Of what class is

JOHN NICHOLSON

the type then? Of none, for truly he stands alone. But he belongs essentially to the school of Henry Lawrence.

I only knocked down the walls of the Bunnoo *forts*.

John Nicholson has since reduced the *people* (the most ignorant, depraved and blood-thirsty in the Punjab) to such a state of good order and respect for the laws, that in the last year of his charge not only was there no murder, burglary, or highway robbery, but not an *attempt* at any of those crimes.

The Bunnoochees, reflecting on their own metamorphosis in the village gatherings under the vines, by the streams they once delighted so to fight for, have come to the conclusion that "the good Mahomedans" of historic ages must have been "just like Nikkul Seyn!" They emphatically approve him as every inch a hâkim. And so he is. It is difficult to describe him. He must be seen. Lord Dalhousie,—no mean judge — perhaps best summed up his high military and administrative qualities, when he called him "a tower of strength." I can only say that I think him equally fit to be Commissioner of a division, or General of an army. Of the strength of his personal character, I will only tell two anecdotes.

1. If you visit either the battle field of Goojarat, or Cheyleanwallah — the country people begin

their narrative of the battles thus, " Nikkul Seyn
stood just *there!*"

2. A brotherhood of Fakeers in Huzara aban-
doned all forms of Asiatic monachism, and commenced the worship of Nikkul Seyn ; — which they
still continue ! Repeatedly they have met John
Nicholson since, and fallen at his feet as their
Gooroo.* He has flogged them soundly on every
occasion, and sometimes imprisoned them ; but the
sect of the Nikkul Seynees remains as devoted as
ever. " Sanguis martyrorum est semen Ecclesiæ."

On the last whipping John Nicholson released
them, on the condition that they would transfer
their adoration to John Becher; — but arrived at
their monastery in Huzara, they once more resumed
the worship of the relentless Nikkul Seyn.

Reynell Tayler

was another of the old set, and the whole set is
proud of him. He set siege to the border fort of
Lukkee, in the war of 1848—49, with a handful of
Mooltânee soldiers, sapped his way regularly up
to the walls, and reduced the garrison to surrender.
He held charge of Bunnoo for two years after annexation, and has published the best account of
that district. His character is so *round* and perfect in its goodness, that one is almost as provoked
with him, as the Athenians with Aristides.

He got a right manly slash down his face, in
charging the Sikh cavalry at Moodkee, or his gentleness and goodness would be worthy of a woman.

* Religious or spiritual guide.

Such were the instruments used by Sir Henry Lawrence. How much England owes him at this moment who shall say ? I will try to recount what the early Punjab Administration has to thank him for, and here again I am greatly assisted by the kindness of Colonel Edwardes.

First.—The men he had about him ; and the high standard of public duty, zeal, personal exertion, and love of the people of the country with which he inspired them. These were the nucleus of the new Administration.

Secondly.—The personal confidence of all classes in a Government over which Sir Henry presided, It was soon known to the Sikhs and chiefs of all kinds that the Governor-General was determined to reduce the Punjab into a British Province, and that John Lawrence, with the aid of George Christian the Secretary to the Board of Administration, would push on vigorously the great change.—Sir Henry interposed with equal vigour, and worked for a transition instead of a revolution.—He eased off every falling interest with the tender compassion of a friend who had known the class in better days. He got a little more for every one. He fought every losing battle for the old chiefs and jaghire dars with entire disregard for his own interest, and at last left the Punjab, to use Colonel Edwardes' words, " dented all over with defeats and disapprovals, honourable scars in the eyes of the bystanders."

Thirdly.—Colonel Edwardes believed that Sir Henry was the proposer of the disarming of the people of the Punjab. Whoever originated this important step, I know Sir Henry cordially enforced and approved of it.

Fourthly.—He raised the Punjab Irregular Force. Lord Dalhousie gave him *all* the appointments. This is the force which took so leading a part in the siege of Delhi, and without which it is not too much to say that we could hardly have effected the reduction of that mutinous stronghold.

Fifthly.—He originated jail reform in the Punjab, abolished the "night chain" and other abominations, introduced in-door labour, and placed all the prisons of the province under one Inspector. His *personal* labours in this matter, going from jail to jail, rooting out abuses, rising even at midnight to visit the prisoners' barracks, thus inspiring his civil subordinates with the idea of "kindness to the captive"; all this evinced the strength and reality of his feelings of humanity. Sir Henry was pre-eminently the friend of *the man who is down;* thieves and convicts not excepted. In all and every good work of this nature he was ably supported by Mr. Montgomery, but Sir Henry had long been at this labour of love before Montgomery came to the Punjab as Commissioner of Lahore.

Lastly (I will not dilute the following note of Colonel Edwardes by a word of my own).

" What distinguished the Punjab Administration in India, was *the simplicity of the Courts of Justice,* their cheapness, accessibility, and promptness; the exclusion of Vakeels; the confronting of the real parties; the arbitration by Punchâyuts.

" I believe that this was *very largely* due to Sir Henry. He was not intimately acquainted with the organisation of the Courts of the North Western Provinces, but in his duties of Revenue Surveyor, had gathered the impression, in village talks, &c. &c., that those Courts were hard of approach, technical in operation, and expensive even in their happiest issues! It fell in, therefore, with all his instincts to avoid these results in the Punjab machinery; and when the Code was being drawn up his vote was strong for simplicity, and expedition, and publicity. In this matter he was certainly *not alone*, for John knew the weaknesses of the system in which he had been raised *still better* than Henry, and was resolved to have a much simpler procedure. I am under the idea that we owe it to John that the revenue, civil and criminal functions, were united in the district officers, which is practically the key-stone of our arch. That came of John knowing the details, and seeing his way to the remedy. The Code in fact was drawn up by John, and owes its working efficiency to him. But what I mean is, that Sir Henry was ever at John's elbow, calling out for the great principles of cheap justice.

" Besides this, he was for ever talking the new officers into his own views; and influencing them to live among the people, to do as many cases under trees, and as few under the punkah, as possible; to ride about their districts and see and hear for themselves, instead of through the police and

Omlah, and his cheery earnest way of doing this, his glad praise of any rough and ready officer, and his indignant contempt for all skulks, idlers, and *nimmuk-hurâm*, drew *models* on young fellows' minds which they went forth and copied in their administrations — it sketched a *faith*, and begot a *school*, and they are both living things to this day. I have no hesitation in saying that he has exercised the greatest personal influence for good of all the men in the Punjab government."

It will not be supposed, from the above remarks, that I wish to disparage the labours and efforts of other men, and to eulogise the dead at the expense of the living. We owe it to Lord Dalhousie that three such men as the two Lawrences and Montgomery exercised so vast an influence over the twelve millions of the Punjab.

His Lordship placed at the Board of Administration, Henry Lawrence, as well as John Lawrence, and Robert Montgomery.

England, or rather Ireland, may well be proud of such sons as these. Five and thirty years back this remarkable trio were playfellows at a little school in the North of Ireland. Five years ago they formed the Board which ruled the destinies of the Punjab, and devised (with the aid of Mr. Mansel and under the valuable auspices of Lord Dalhousie) that scheme of government which must one day dominate over the Indian Peninsula.

Now, the one rules over the Punjab, having justly been hailed, within the last twelve months, the Saviour of Upper India.

The other, equally honoured and beloved by his countrymen, is stilling the troubled sea of insurrection in Oude.

The third, now alas, beyond the reach of human praise, lives only here in the hearts of his friends, and the gratitude of the English Nation.*

---

* Sir H. Lawrence was as well suited for the duty of *pacification* as was Sir John for the work of administration. Conciliation was the forte of one, governing was the instinct of the other. Therefore, when the work of conciliation was over, Lord Dalhousie showed a wise discretion (in my humble opinion) when he left the task of mere administration in the hands of Sir John Lawrence.

CHAP. V.

To return to Agra. On the 30th May, at midnight, Mr. Muir and Dr. Farquhar called at the Candaharee Bagh, to tell us that a company of the regiment of Native Infantry sent out to relieve the guard over the treasury at Muttra, had mutinied, shooting down their officer, and then pursuing the course — now a routine one — of firing the houses of the English and breaking the prisons.

Mr. Colvin, with the advice of Mr. Drummond, the Magistrate, had at length wisely determined to disarm our two regiments of Sepoys. It became necessary for us, in the event of any outbreak on the part of these men, some of whom were posted at the Central Jail, in the heart of the Civil Station, to protect ourselves and the many defenceless Christian men, women, and children around. My colleague, Mr. Morgan, kindly allowed his house to be made a rendezvous in case of danger. Notices were sent round, and early in the morning of Sunday, some hundreds of all ranks and ages had congregated at the Candaharee Bagh, the men armed with swords and revolvers, the women generally dragging children and ayahs. We fell naturally under the command of Colonel Fraser, Chief Engineer of the North-Western Provinces, a fine old officer who had won his decoration as C.B. by an act of heroism in Burmah during the last campaign. Musquets and ammunition were served out, a chain of sentries posted, and the house began to be transformed from an elegant garden pavilion into a rough uncouth-looking fortress. In the military lines, the native regiments were drawn up on parade, a battery of artillery, under Captain D'Oyley, and the 3rd Europeans under Colonel Riddell, in a position to enforce obedience. The word "pile arms" was given. There was a moment of hesitation, a look of discontent. The officers sternly reiterated the order. Silent and sullen, the Sepoys obeyed—piled their arms, and were marched off to the lines. The 44th and 67th Regiments, whose colours had waved from the Indus to the Brahmapootra, were no more.

On examining the musquets, many were found loaded with ball. It was afterwards well known, that on this very Sunday morning, the Sepoys had conspired to overpower the European regiment when in Church, to rush upon the guns, and then to shoot, plunder and burn from one end of Agra to the other.

Whilst this was passing, five miles away from us, in the cantonments, a less successful manœuvre was executed close at hand. A detachment of the 3rd Europeans was marched suddenly up in front of the company of Sepoys on guard at the jail. The men imagined that an attack was intended, and ran in all directions, carrying their arms, and threatening to shoot any one who came near them. My young friend, Lieutenant Williams, who had left our garrison at Candaharee Bagh to reconnoitre, met some of these men, who began loading their musquets, vociferating and abusing him. Placing his hand in his breast, he told them to fire; on this they slunk away abashed, and most of them eventually gave up their arms, on reaching cantonments.

We were all very glad at Candaharee when Mr. Thornhill, the Secretary to Government, who had been to the cantonments to see the Lieutenant-Governor's order carried out, told us that the regiments had surrendered their arms. I set to work at once, with Colonel Fraser's full consent, to organise a permanent guard for the Candaharee Bagh. Stout English clerks, sun-burnt old soldiers on the pension list, Roman Catholic artillerymen who had fought under Scindia, East Indian sectioners, record keepers and tradesmen,—such was my material. As the Candaharee Bagh was now officially recognised by the Government as one of the chief places of rendezvous in the event of an émeute, I was well supplied with beer and biscuit for the garrison. Hundreds of large water vessels were ranged around the outer verandahs, sand bags were piled. The twelve o'clock gun * was

---

* The distance of the Civil Lines from the Cantonments was so great, that we had a separate gun daily fired at 12 o'clock.

dragged from its wonted site, and placed in a position to command the entrance into the Bagh. Grape shot were extemporised at a neighbouring coachmaker's shop, and, in short, we prepared ourselves to hold out in case of a sudden attack either from Sepoys, town mobs, prisoners, or the revolted regiments from Nusseerabad, which we knew were marching upon Agra.

I also raised, and with the liberal assistance of the Government equipped, a troop of Horse Volunteers. These men were intended by me to act as mounted police and patrols, and in the event of what we all daily and nightly expected, a "rush to the Fort," were to protect and escort the women and children for three miles from the Civil Lines through the city to the Fort. I at first commanded them in person, Major Prendergast kindly consenting to act under my orders. Early in June, with the assistance of Lieutenant Hugo James, who was also attached to the troop, I proceeded to Futtehabad to bring in the ladies and children from Etaweh. Although some person, I know not who, was good enough to send an account of this little expedition to the papers at the time, when an unmerited amount of praise was given to a very ordinary performance, I think it right, in order to subserve my prominent object of describing faithfully the state of the country and people, to sketch the expedition.

A little before sunset on the evening of the 15th June, our little party, consisting of Mr. Phillipps, the Magistrate of Etah, Lieutenant Hugo James, and the troop of thirty or forty Horse Volunteers under my command, marched from the Candaharee Bagh, through the city of Agra, towards Futteha-bad.* Passing the Catholic Church and Convent, we were loudly cheered by the inmates. I recollect nothing of the night march except the astonishing quantity of water which we drank at every well on the road-side. But for the streaming perspiration no human skin could have contained the amount of liquid poured into us. Yet, just at this burn-ing period, our poor countrymen and women were being hunted like wild beasts, *day and night*, all over Upper India.

Before day-break we reached Futtehabad. The citizens were in a state of anxious alarm. The rough Goojurs and Jats from Scindia's side of the Chum-bul, were pouring down upon our villages, plun-dering, burning, and murdering all who resisted. The Thanadar had been surprised by them in a neighbouring village, and with difficulty escaped. A town watch had been hastily organised by the local police. The Tehsildar (native chief of revenue and police) and Moonsiff (native judge) received us with delight into the Tehseel station, a large straggling native fort. Both were in a state of the highest excitement ; they had been repeatedly threatened with a visit from the Trans-Chumbul dacoits; the town was to be looted and their heads stuck upon the walls.

* This town is about twenty-five miles from the Civil Lines in a south-easterly direction. It is situated between the Jumna and the Chumbul rivers.

Soon after our arrival, whilst I was trying to get a short sleep on the Tehsildar's charpoy, an alarm was given. Lights were seen in the distance, there was a sound of men, horses, and carriages. The Tehsildar, putting a cap on his gun, declared that at last the enemy was upon us. It turned out, as I hoped and expected, that the cavalcade approaching consisted of the ladies and children from Etaweh, escorted by a detachment of Sepoys of the Gwalior Contingent, Irregular Cavalry, and some loyal Rajah's match-lock men, under the command of a very spirited and intelligent young Englishman, Mr. W. H. Parker.

As our presence afforded merely a temporary protection to the Tehsildar, I wrote at his request to Luchmun Singh, the chief of the Goojurs, and to another talook-dar in the immediate neighbourhood, for a couple of hundred match-lock men and some horse to assist in maintaining the authority of Government in Futtehabad. Under ordinary circumstances an order of this sort would have been promptly attended to; it was an unpleasant sign of the times that this answer came— "Luchmun Singh was much afraid that his men would join the marauders in their meditated attack on the town and Tehseel station." The fact was, these men had heard of the revolt of the Gwalior Contingent, and considered that the days of the British rule were numbered, and that in self-defence it was necessary for them to keep on good terms with Scindia's subjects.

The jemadar of the guard of Sepoys very sulkily counted over the ladies, children, and nurses, to me, and from his surly conduct I conclude that he had already heard how his brethren in arms at Gwalior had been rioting in the blood of our countrymen. It was a great happiness to have the party safe, and to conduct them without any alarm to Agra, on the night of June 16th. On reaching the Candaharee Bagh, we heard first that the Gwalior Contingent had mutinied, secondly that Delhi had fallen to our arms. The first report was unhappily too true; the last, to our sorrow, proved false.

As our fate at Agra depended much on the conduct of Scindia and his Contingent force, I turn to notice their conduct.

Gwalior is about seventy miles south-west of Agra, on the great road to Bombay. The Contingent force, of which the greater part was posted at Gwalior, consisted of five companies of artillery, with a magazine and siege train (3rd class), two cavalry and seven infantry regiments, under the command of Brigadier Ramsay. When the mutiny at Meerut broke out, the Lieutenant-Governor at once applied at Gwalior for cavalry and artillery. There was nothing in the conduct of the men who came to Agra to make us suppose that they would separate themselves from the Sepoys in general; nay, they rather piqued themselves on belonging to the army, and, as is usual with Contingent forces, looked up with respect to the regulars. If then the Bengal army was turning against us, we had no reason to hope that the

Gwalior Contingent would continue on our side. True, their officers, with that over-weening yet manly confidence to which nothing but a bullet could put a period, believed in their men. Nobody else did; certainly not Major Macpherson, Political Agent at the court of Scindia. His eyes were soon opened. The Maharaja told him plainly enough that the soldiers of the Contingent would soon follow the example of Meerut and Delhi. In nightly conference it was determined to rise, burn, and slay. Women and children alone were to be spared. In the meantime, until the fitting day arrived, the British officers were to be cajoled. And so it was. There was no reserve on the awful subject of the mutiny. Officers freely talked to their men; and their native subordinates, who in the lines were settling the propitious day and hour for cutting the throats of every Englishman, boasted, with tears in their eyes, how they would revenge the murders of Delhi and Meerut; and cursed the villains whose example they had determined to follow. Our officers would not allow themselves to suspect the men who had served them so long and so well. Meerut, Delhi, Allyghur, Muttra, had fallen, all around was falling, yet they refused to believe that their men, though of the same stock and stuff, could fail. They were ready to seal their faith, not only with their blood, but with what they prized far dearer, the blood of their wives and children. These true-hearted, faithful English gentlemen could not discern the mainspring of the machinery which was at work around them. What the Sepoys wanted was, to transfer their allegiance from England to the Mogul or to Scindia, or whoever might employ them, at once, as a body, complete and in perfect organisation. A rabble was to be picked up in every suburb; but an army, in a full state of discipline and equipment—this was a prize for which any monarch might bid high. It was, therefore, the policy of the native officers not only to conceal their treachery, but also to maintain to the last moment every sign and mark of the most perfect subordination and discipline.

We at Agra watched Gwalior anxiously. I had particular reasons for disquiet. Not only my friends, Major Macpherson and his sister, Mrs. Innes, were there in danger, but my kinsman, Major Raikes, had taken a part of his regiment, the 1st Gwalior Cavalry, to Mynpoorie, leaving his wife and infant with Major and Mrs. Blake, at Gwalior.

It had been decided by the military authorities that the ladies should not be removed, as the Sepoys were considered worthy of trust. So when the mutiny broke out, these delicate creatures were exposed to the fury of the revolt. On my return to Agra from Futtehabad, on hearing that the Political Agent, Major Macpherson, and several other refugees, had arrived from Gwalior, I wrote to him, enclosing a letter to my cousin, from my wife. I received the following reply from Mrs. Innes, the sister of Major Macpherson. It will serve to depict the scenes passing near us at this moment.

"I opened your note, as my brother is asleep, not ill, but much exhausted by exposure on the journey and anxiety.

"I deeply grieve that I must return Mrs. Raikes' note. We have some hope there may yet be good news of her, but we have reason to fear the worst. It is not certainty. Mrs. Raikes may have escaped, but Major Blake, in whose house she was, we know was mortally wounded at the beginning; and of Mrs. Blake and Mrs. Raikes we have been able to hear nothing. It is so utterly heart-breaking that I cannot venture to let myself realise it yet. We and many others have been mercifully preserved, but there are no fewer than eight ladies still unaccounted for, and that at least four or five of these were shot we have too little reason to doubt. However, some of them may have been defended and hidden. I had just written a note to Mrs. Raikes, but think it better to send this to you. It is so miserable a story that either to think or write of it is at present too much.

"Will you tell Mrs. Raikes that I should be very grateful to her for any change of dress she could afford me? Any sort of old thing until I can make other arrangements. I scarcely know what I have written, but only require an hour's sleep to make me all right.

"I hope you and Mrs. Raikes are as well as you can be in such sad and trying times, &c."

On the next day we had the happiness of receiving our cousin. Like hundreds of our country-women, she had been driven rudely from her home, exposed to the fury of an Indian sun and to the jests of the Sepoy rabble. Happier than many, her husband as yet was safe, and her child, and her courage had never failed for a moment.

She described her adventures thus:—On the afternoon of Sunday, 13th June, a building near the Mess House had been burnt; the Sepoys rushing to put out the flames, the usual trick to avert suspicion. Some, however, were overheard to say, we shall have a finer blaze to-night. Late in the evening, as Mrs. Blake and Mrs. Raikes were going to bed, shots were fired, flames began to ascend on all sides. The critical moment had come. The Contingent was in mutiny. Guards were posted by the mutineers on the roads to shoot down every officer who attempted to pass. Major Blake, a man who had devoted his whole life to his men, galloping towards the lines was shot down by the soldiers of another regiment. His own men, strange to say, wept as they watched his life-blood oozing away, and called loudly for medical aid when all aid was too late. When Major Blake rode off, his servants, seeing a body of mutineers coming down to the house, hastily concealed the ladies, child, and native wet nurse in a stable. The Reverend Mr. Coopland* and his wife afterwards joined them. Subsequently they were obliged to take shelter in a small outhouse. The Sepoy wretches, too cowardly to come in at the

* Military Chaplain at Gwalior.

door, got upon the roof and fired down. All were driven out. The Sepoys spared the women but seized the clergyman. He said, "I am not a fighting man, but a padre." * So much the worse, was their reply. He was shot down. Some men of the infantry, after the ladies had been deprived of their rings, escorted them to Scindia's Palace, which is some miles from the Cantonment. All the ladies, except Mrs. Stewart, were saved. She with her husband was murdered, I believe by the artillerymen.

Sometimes in covered carts, sometimes walking, these delicate creatures, with little but their sleeping dresses on them, without covering on their heads, had reached Agra.

The following letter, addressed about this time to me, by Captain D'Oyly, will be read with great interest by all who remember how nobly, all mangled and bleeding from his death wound, he fought his battery on the memorable 5th of July.

" I have just seen Campbell, and have had a long chat with him regarding the two artillery ladies, who, with their families, are still supposed to be at or near Gwalior.

" It would appear, that when Campbell yesterday morning was pushing on towards Gwalior, to meet his wife, &c., he fell in with a Sowar of the 1st Regiment Gwalior Irregulars (Alexander's). This man told him that he had heard from another native, that both Mrs. Hawkins and Mrs. Stewart, with

---

* The word commonly used all over India for a minister of religion.

their children, were safe, and were under the protection of the Maharaja. Campbell says that he
has no reason whatever to doubt this man's story.

"He is of opinion that no attempt had better be
made by Europeans to assist in rescuing, protecting, or escorting these two ladies, that, most likely
if the people under whose charge they now are,
heard that a party of 'Gora-log' (Europeans) were
coming down to rescue the ladies, they might get
exasperated, and destroy the persons whom they
are now protecting ; under these circumstances, I
think we have no alternative but to follow Campbell's advice.

"I fear, therefore, we must leave them to their
fate, hoping for the best, and should any tidings be
received to the effect that these ladies had left the
places where they now may be, and were attempting
to get into Agra, then the services of a party of
your Horse might be of great use."

The following note also is characteristic of the
spirit of my gallant young friend, Lieutenant Hugo
James.

" Many thanks for allowing me to peruse D'Oyly's
letter; perhaps Campbell's advice is the best.

"However, I shall always be ready to move out
at a moment's notice, should it be necessary."

As the sad month of June passed on, the Government determined to raise militia, horse and foot,
and place the levies under military law and military
leaders. Mr. Harington came to me and said
that it was considered in the cantonments that it
would be conducive to the public good, if I would

resign the command of my Horse to Major Prendergast, to be employed in the cantonments. Suffering as I was from low fever, and distracted by private calamity, I was obliged to confess that I had no qualities left in me to compensate for my ignorance of military tactics. I accordingly drew up a short address to my men, thanking them for their services, and informing them that it had been intimated to me that the formation of one strong corps of mounted militia, with experienced military men both as *first* and second in command, would conduce more to the public good, than the existing divided corps at the civil lines and the cantonments. I therefore resigned the command in favour of Major Prendergast.

I retained the charge of the defences at Candaharee Bagh.

I sent my address to Mr. Harington, who wrote, " I am sure the men will be much pleased with it" (the address). " I will explain to Mr. Colvin the circumstances under which you have relinquished the command of your gallant little band, and can have no doubt that he will again thank you for the good service which you have rendered to the state, and applaud the public spirit by which you have been actuated throughout."

The Lieutenant-Governor, in the course of the month, honoured me and Major Prendergast by an official acknowledgment of our services. I regret to add that disease, brought on by fatigue and exposure, ere long hurried Major Prendergast into an untimely grave. He died, like many others who had been exposed to excessive heat and hard work, from cholera, soon after our retirement to the Fort. Courteous, prudent, and brave, no officer was more popular, and more justly respected by his men. After his death, Mr. Vere, a spirited gentleman in the customs department, was placed in charge of the corps, with a Lieutenant's commission. It was still doing good service when I left Agra.

During the latter half of the month of June, Colonel Fraser, Mr. Harington, and the Judges of the Sudder Court, had occasion to remonstrate very earnestly with the Lieutenant-Governor with regard to his policy. I have already hinted that the Police at Agra, as at other places in the North-Western Provinces, was more feared than respected by most men who wished well to the British Government. In the first place, all over Upper India, every man who had a pretension to an uniform, who knew any thing of drill or a firelock, set himself up for a Sepoy. Now, the Agra Police not only were dressed, drilled, and armed, but also had an enormous supply of balled ammunition served out to them by the Magistrate, the Honourable Robert Drummond. This gentleman, in the early days of the revolt, had acquired the confidence of all men, by his courage, zeal, and activity. But, as time wore on, and matters assumed a graver complexion, he, Englishman like, fell into the same error which I have attributed to the military officers of Gwalior. Nothing could shake his faith in his men. Unfortunately these men — I mean his leading and confidential agents—were all, without exception, Ma-

homedans, and the Mahomedans were all, or nearly
all, traitors thirsting for English blood. — So it
happened that at Agra we found ourselves in the
hands of a Magistrate who was himself, as we all
thought, victimized by a clique of cunning blood-
thirsty Mahomedans. The high spirit and courage
of Mr. Drummond gave weight to his counsels, his
position as Magistrate of Agra gave him opportunity. He alone could, under our constitution,
act: his superiors, with the exception of Mr. Colvin,
having only the power to protest or expostulate.
His principle was to show no sign of fear, and he
considered every precaution to be a sign of fear.
The Lieutenant-Governor, worn out by incessant
fatigue, depressed by daily tidings of disaster, the
victim of approaching disease, put himself, I may
almost say entirely, into Mr. Drummond's hands.
High-minded, frank, and open, he naturally preferred to trust men rather than suspect them. He
trusted Drummond, as under ordinary circumstances
he might well do, and Drummond trusted his
Mahomedan subordinates, whose object was to destroy him and every other Englishman in Agra.
At the invitation of the Police, as was generally believed, the whole of the mutineers from Neemuch,
horse and foot, with a powerful artillery, were
marching steadily upon us. The Police cut off our
communications, opposed the officers who were engaged in victualling the Fort, and by their insolent
demeanour, daily proved more plainly what was
passing in their minds.

Colonel Fraser, Mr. Harington, Mr. Vansittart,

E 3

my colleagues, and I, watched their proceedings
with anxiety, and remonstrated with the Lieutenant-Governor.   We felt convinced that when the
Neemuch mutineers attacked the Station, the Police
would cut off the retreat to the Fort, and we urged,
not that we ourselves should be admitted, nor even
our wives and families, but that the schools, the
convents, the old and infirm, and those who were
too poor to have any vehicle, should be allowed to take up their quarters within the walls of
the Fort.   For ourselves, we determined to hold
the Candaharee Bagh to the last moment, and most
of the ladies of the Civil Lines, with their children
and nurses, slept there every night.*

It was not till the end of the month that Mr.
Colvin consented to allow the helpless part of the
Christian population to retire within the Fort.   It
was forbidden to send in any property beyond the
sort of allowance which a French Customs House
Officer at Calais or Marseilles, passes under the term
of a *sac de nuit*.†   Hence, the loss and destruction of books, furniture, archives, records, public
and private, and the ruin of hundreds of families.
This loss might have been avoided, if in the beginning of the mutiny, as at Lahore, precautions

---

* Thanks to Mr. Morgan's kindness, every woman and child
was welcome.   The garden was filled with tents, in which, as
well as in the house, the women and children slept, whilst the
men took their share of the duty as sentries, &c.

† This prohibition was slightly relaxed when almost too late
to benefit the public.   Boxes were admitted on a written order
from the officer in charge of the Fort.

had been taken at once. Our truest courage was to be prepared for the worst. I am not aware that any precautions could eventually have saved our houses at Agra from destruction, but invaluable property might have been preserved, if early permission had been given to place it within the precincts of the Fort. The work of victualling might have proceeded at one gate, whilst private and public property was admitted at another.

CHAP. VI.

THE RETIREMENT TO THE FORT.

THE month of July had set in.   Colonel Fraser,
considering the Candaharee Bagh no longer ten-
able, had left us, and taken a small house under
the walls of the Fort.   Residents in Cantonments
looked at us in the Civil Lines, as doomed men.
The fine frame of Mr. Colvin was sinking under the
ravages of disease, yet he persisted in attending to
every detail of business; whilst he acknowledged
to me that the load of responsibility, the agony
caused by the sufferings and dangers of his officers
at every station in Upper India, was too much for
human endurance, he resolutely watched every
detail of public business.   Even now, if I wanted
a sword or a pistol from the magazine, Mr. Colvin's
counter-signature was necessary.

His cares might well press hard on the strongest
frame.   The fabric of Government was falling
to pieces, all over the North-Western Provinces.
High officials, accustomed to command the obedience of millions, were hiding in the jungles, hunted
by their own guards, or holding desperate positions
against hopeless odds.   One cry for help arose from
east to west.   Vibart and Robert Thornhill, at

Furuckabad,* with a score of men armed with
fowling pieces, were defying whole regiments,
keeping thousands at bay; Major Raikes and John
Powel holding out against hope at Mynpoorie.
Probyn, the Magistrate of Furuckabad, hidden in
the hut of a friendly Zemindar. Cocks, Watson,
young Harington, and a dozen English gentlemen
at Allygurh, with mutineers on every side of
them. In Rohilcund, Rajpootana, Cawnpore, and
Bundelcund silence, too often the silence of the
grave. At Futtehpore, Robert Tucker defending
himself single-handed against the villains whom he
had refused to suspect, and dying only when his
last bullet was expended. And so all over the
country, the English were at bay. Mr. Colvin
expected much from his subordinates, but he had
a heart to feel for their sufferings. He could not
bear to give up station after station to anarchy,
neither could he quietly see his trusted friends and
officers butchered like sheep. The struggle con-
sumed him. " The wrath of God is upon us," he
exclaimed, " if we retire into the Fort."

Nevertheless, early in July events hurried on,
which drove Mr. Colvin and every other living
Christian, man, woman, or child at Agra, and
within a radius of a hundred miles round about,
into the Fort, glad enough to lose their property,
and seek the only shelter for life now remaining. Mutiny, like a belt of fire, surrounded us.

* The scraps in French which we used to get from Furuckabad asking for help, which Mr. Colvin was unable to give,
were heartrending.

Still we held in Agra a straggling position, from east to west some six miles long, with only one regiment of European soldiers, and a few undisciplined militia. Each day brought the Neemuch mutineers nearer. Regiments or detachments, hitherto faithful, were reported one after the other in mutiny. To bring our dangers to a climax, the Joudpore Legion, consisting of some two thousand men of all arms, were ordered into the Station just as the Neemuch mutineers arrived within a couple of marches of Agra. This last move brought matters to a crisis. I asked the opinion of Major M'Leod, Military Secretary to the Lieut.-Governor, and Captain Nixon, who had just come in to Government House from Bhurtpore, as to whether we in the Civil Lines, in the immediate vicinity of the Jail, with its four thousand desperadoes, and four miles from the Cantonments, could safely keep our wives and children there any longer. The answer was,—No. Thus, about the last day of June, we took the women and children to the Fort, to exchange their spacious and well-furnished houses for any hut that might be allotted them. I felt it a relief to see them comparatively safe, but the ladies themselves begged to be allowed to stay out with us, and to continue to share our dangers at Candaharee Bagh. Here I pause to offer a tribute of admiration to the courage and endurance of our English women. Throughout the mutiny self seemed forgotten, anxieties, if vented, were only for the husband, the brother, or the friend.

Up to the 4th of July, with Mr. Harington and

my colleagues, I continued to sleep outside the Fort.
On the night of the 3rd, we held our last watch at
the Candaharee Bagh. Restless and sleepless, from
a fever which had for some time past been pro-
gressing upon me, I watched the sleepers around.
There lay the member for Agra, of the Legislative
Council of India, half dressed, a sword by his bed
side, a gun in the corner, and a revolver under his
pillow.   Those gaunt, unshaven, weary-looking
men by his side are the Judges of the Sudder
Court. For six weeks they have been watching
the rising flood of revolt, which had now risen more
than breast high. Will they ever sleep with a roof
of their own over their heads again?

On the 4th, we all spent part of the day in the
Fort. I was prostrate with fever, and unable to
lift up my head. The forms of office went on, and
though the Court was closed and I had no home
to go to, save a barrack in the Fort, I considered
it right to obtain a regular certificate of my condition.*

Owing to my illness, I am unable to report the
occurrences of the 4th as an eye-witness. I remember, however, that my cousin, Major Raikes,
who had just come in from Mynpoorie, his men in
the eleventh hour having deserted him, went to
Mr. Colvin, or the Brigadier, or both, with my

---

* " I hereby certify that Mr. Raikes, C.S., is suffering from an
attack of fever, for which I have prescribed, and I consider it
necessary that he should remain quiet at home for a few days.
                                " S. CLARK, Assistant Surgeon.
" July 4th, 1857."

hearty concurrence, to urge that the Joudpoor
Legion should be at once disarmed. No reasonable man could doubt that they would take the
first favourable moment to turn upon us, and the
mutineers from Neemuch were already almost
within sight of Agra. In the afternoon of the 4th,
the Legion broke into mutiny, murdered the European Sergeant-Major, and went off to join the
Sepoy army, now within a few miles of Cantonments. The Lieutenant-Governor, who for some
weeks past had spent the nights in Cantonments,
came into the Fort. The Civil Lines were by this
time nearly deserted. All held their breath, in-
tent upon the coming struggle, when the fate of
Agra was to be decided.

It is no part of my intention to chronicle battles.
Every one knows that on the 5th July, Brigadier
Polwhele led out his men to attack the mutineers,
that after a hard fight he retired into the Fort
surrounded by clouds of the enemy's cavalry,
whilst their infantry and artillery moved off in the
opposite direction towards Muttra and Delhi.

The Brigadier has been blamed; I presume because he was not successful. For all this, he was
a true soldier. We have time now to consider the
difficulties of his position. And who can deny that
they were overwhelming? In the first place he
considered it his duty to obey implicitly Mr. Colvin, who had been invested with the powers of the
Governor-General. He carried out a policy in the
matter of the preparation of the Fort, for instance,
to which he himself was opposed. He might

possibly have resisted more earnestly, on this and
other points, the wishes of the Lieutenant-Governor, but he is not justly obnoxious to the sort
of blame which has been lavished on him, merely
because he feared, in a time of military convulsion,
to throw overboard the Civil Government. His
difficulties were enormous. It early became evi-
dent that contingents, legions, levies, every sort of
military organisation, except the personal guards
of Scindia, would join their Sepoy brethren and
turn against us. The more troops we had, save
our one weak European regiment and battery, the
greater our danger. A powerful enemy threatened
us from without; treachery grew up within and
around us. The Mahratta guards were withdrawn.

Brigadier Polwhele determined to strike a blow
at the enemy, with 500 men against 5000. He
struck and failed. He could not command success, but I should be sorry to say that he did not
deserve it.

Owing to my rank in the service, I was allowed
to occupy one of the best quarters in the Fort, in
the tiled barracks. We had three rooms, each
about fourteen feet square. No windows, but a
wooden door to each, and a veranda on either side.
Our party, besides Mrs. Raikes and myself, consisted of two families, the Reverend Valpy French,
his wife and two children; Major Raikes, Mrs.
Raikes and one child: there were also two wet-
nurses, and three women servants. One room
served for the gentlemen at night, and for our

dining-room at day. The other two rooms were given up to the ladies and children. It was hot and uncomfortable, as may be supposed, but not intolerable. We put up punkahs, and hired little native Christian boys to pull them. Many of our friends had much more confinement to bear.

From my sick bed in the afternoon of Sunday, the 5th July, I heard the cannonade, which lasted for nearly two hours. There was a commotion in the veranda, and my wife came in to tell me that Mr. French, who had watched the battle from the ramparts, reported our discomfiture. The English, surrounded by clouds of cavalry, were retreating slowly towards the Fort, ever and anon facing and firing volleys at their pursuers.

Then came the rush of weary soldiers to the Canteen, which was close to our room, and in the same barrack. Bloody, thirsty, covered with dust and smoke, the soldiers clamoured for drink. Beer, tea, wine and water were hastily given them by the ladies of our party. I could overhear their remarks. " Ah my chummie! my townie!" said one, whose comrade had been left dead on the battle field. " Faith! and the Major (Major Thomas) went at 'em grand," said another. The long string of hospital litters passed through the Fort gates. The gallant D' Oyley was carried in to die. Young Williams was undergoing the amputation of a leg in the hospital. Richard Oldfield, Under-Secretary to Government, was brought faint, and steeped in blood, to his young wife. I had a small tent near the barrack; in this two wounded officers were lodged.

A line of fire in the Cantonments showed the course of the retreating enemy. Barracks, private houses, bazaars, all were in a blaze.

On the 6th and 7th July, our tired men were not allowed to leave the Fort. My own house and a large part of the Civil Lines were not burnt until after the night of the 6th. Then the natives, who had hitherto protected our property, seeing that we did not leave the Fort, gave us up. The King of Delhi was proclaimed in the public places, and every remaining house was burnt and plundered. Few servants were to be found, we had to draw water from the wells inside the Fort, and were badly supplied with food. But all this passed away when, on or about the 8th, a military demonstration was made, and some guns and infantry marched through the city. At once there was a reaction. The people flocked to the Fort with provisions; washermen, water-carriers, tailors, shepherds, cooks and sweepers came pouring in to help their masters, who were generally too glad to see their domestics to ask many questions as to how the days since the 5th had been passed.

I, for one, do not blame these men for retiring quietly out of the fray, and standing aloof at a moment when it would have been certain death to them to pursue any other course. If they came near the Fort, our soldiers fired at them; if they showed at a distance from the Fort any disposition to help the Christians, the mutineers and Mahomedan rabble would have murdered them at once.

Some few servants, generally Mahomedans, behaved ill, and joined with the prisoners and rabble in the plunder of their masters, but most of the menial class continued faithful. On my own establishment, one old and favoured servant, a Mahomedan butler, behaved ill amongst about fifty. The rest were singularly devoted and faithful, and followed me in all my subsequent wanderings up to the Punjab and down to Calcutta.

CHAP. VII.

THREE miles from the Civil Lines, and one mile from Cantonments, on a gentle curve overhanging the right bank of the river Jumna, stands the Fort of Agra: with its high red sandstone walls, deep ditch, and drawbridge, it looks now—what it really was when the Emperor Akber rebuilt it in 1570 —impregnable.

Within are the Palace, with its gilded cupolas, and rich tracery of gold and blue enamel, on which Akber lavished millions; the Motee Musjid, or Pearl Mosque, of pure marble, and dazzling white-ness; the Arsenal, and other public buildings. Such is the Fort of Agra. When visiting the Palace or the Motee Musjid in happier days, how little had any sight-seeing Englishman expected that within those walls the shattered remnants of his nation would one day be crowded?

Yet so it was. Whatever remained unscathed, from Meerut to Allahabad, either of Englishmen or of their works, was conglomerated here. Here were the remnants of the record of survey and revenue settlement, that great work on which heaps of money and the best energies of our best

F

men had been lavished for a quarter of a century. Here were the only munitions of war, the only instruments of art or materials of science, which remained to us.

In huts hastily prepared, amongst the galleries and gateways of the old Palace of the Emperors, a motley crowd assembled. Matted screens were set up along the marble corridors which in Akber's time were hung with the silks of Persia and the brocades of Benares.

Under this shade not only was every part of our British Isles represented, but we had also unwilling delegates from many parts of Europe and America. Nuns from the banks of the Garonne and the Loire, priests from Sicily and Rome, missionaries from Ohio and Basle, mixed with rope dancers from Paris, and pedlars from Armenia. Besides these we had Calcutta Baboos, and Parsee merchants. Although all the Christians alike were driven by the mutinous legions into the Fort, the circumstances of the multitude were as various as their races.

There were men who had endured more than all the afflictions of Job, who had lost like him not only their sons, daughters, and every thing they possessed, but who also mourned over the fate of wife, mother, and sister! Reserved, silent, solitary amongst the crowd, they longed either to live alone with their grief, or to quench the fire within by some hurried act of vengeance or despair.

Some few there were, on the other hand, who secretly rejoiced in the troubles of the Christian race, who fattened on their spoil and waited only to betray them if opportunity should offer.

The mass had lost their property: the householder his houses, the merchant his money, the shopkeeper his stores. Part, however, was saved: you could buy millinery or perfumery, but not cheese, beer, wine, nor tobacco.

In short, we had to rough it at Agra, to bear discomfort and privation; but as the bazaars soon opened and generally remained open, we had no real hardships to undergo. If our army retired from before the walls of Delhi, or if the Gwalior Contingent, with their artillery and siege train, made up their minds to attack us, as was constantly threatened, then we might be subjected to a siege. Havelock wrote us that he hoped to come soon; in the meantime, added he, " let Agra be as Julalabad."

Early in September, Mr. Colvin asked me to prepare a plan for the restoration of the Police in the North-Western Provinces, and I submitted a note on the subject ; on the 7th, I called to talk over the matter, but found the Lieutenant-Governor too ill to attend to business. On Wednesday, 9th, to our great sorrow he died, and on the next day, I, as pall bearer, paid my last tribute of respect to his memory. After ruling over the fairest provinces of India in her palmiest days, he died without secure possession of an acre of ground beyond the Fort, and his body was interred within the walls— an abler pen than mine has done justice to his public and private character. I will merely repeat what I have said already. He perished, because in spite of the entreaties of his friends, he would persist in continual mental labour, when his physical state demanded complete repose. The Governor-General paid a just tribute to his name and memory.*

On the 13th September, Major Raikes' child died. She had been snatched by her mother from the bayonets of the Gwalior soldiers, and, I think, had never recovered from the exposure of the journey from Gwalior to Agra.

My own health, too, broken by an insidious fever, long since contracted in the Punjab, entirely failed, and my medical advisers expressed their opinion that a change to an European climate was necessary.

Here I resume my journal.

"*September* 18*th*. — Noon. A message from a banker at Khoorja to another at Hatrass as follows: —

"'Company's rupees are current in Delhi City, though not in the Fort. Two thousand Lucknow rupees received here, and will be sent to Coel† to-morrow.' The meaning of this cautiously worded despatch was clear enough. The English had got into the city of Delhi, and some of the mutineers had run as far as Khoorja." ‡

---

* See "Calcutta Gazette Extraordinary." Notification, dated 19th September, 1857.

† Allygurh.

‡ A town on the grand trunk road, between Delhi and Allygurh.

From Delhi also, came other mutineers along the right bank of the Jumna, in vast numbers, to Muttra. There they divided; part went across the river by a bridge of boats, which they constructed, and marched towards Furuckabad. Others struck across, in a south-westerly direction, to Dholpore, and, combining with some of the Gwalior Contingent and other rebels and mutineers, decided to attack Agra.

I take up my journal again.

" *September* 21*st.* — To-day, the news from Delhi is decidedly good. We took the magazines and vast stores, including 120 guns, on the 16th, and are gradually taking the city. The Gwalior accounts are better. I feel, for the first time, as if we might, without presumption, look forward with some confidence to the future.

" *October* 3*rd.*—The mutineers are leaving Muttra.

" *Wednesday,* 7*th.*—The mutineers from Dholpore are moving in this direction with heavy guns.

" *Thursday,* 8*th.* — Last evening, Major Montgomery was ordered in with his detachment. He has done excellent service between this and Allygurh. He is much disgusted that Colonel Fraser (who has been appointed to act as Chief Commissioner, with full civil and military authority) will not allow him, with about 150 men and two guns, to attack the mutineers, who have some 10,000, and ten or twelve guns. We hear that Greathed's column will be here by Saturday.

" *Saturday,* 10*th.* — We went to the Shah

Boorj (Royal Bastion) this morning, to see Colonel
Greathed's moveable column cross the bridge.
Sikhs, lancers, three batteries of horse artillery,
and the skeletons of two Queen's regiments. This
column came in by long forced marches, owing to
an express sent out by Colonel Fraser. From the
bastion we went down to the Delhi Gate. The
Queen's 8th passed within three yards of us.
'Those dreadful-looking men must be Afghans,'
said a lady to me, as they slowly and wearily
marched by. I did not discover they were Englishmen until I saw a short clay pipe in the
mouth of nearly the last man. My heart bled to
see these jaded miserable objects, and to think of
all they must have suffered since May last, to
reduce fine Englishmen to such worn, sun-dried
skeletons. 'Sure, your honour,' said an Irish serjeant, ' and it's the air has been too strong for 'em;
they was well enough in Delhi amongst the stink,
but coming out into the fresh country air has been
too much for 'em.' I did not argue the point, but
thought that the damp nights and hot days, with
long marches and constant fights, had probably
done more harm to the poor fellows than the
'fresh country air.' They wore the Khakee, or
dust-coloured Sikh Irregular uniform. We tried to
follow the column in the carriage, but found such
a stoppage from baggage near the Umur Singh
Gate, that we turned back. Just after breakfast
garrison orders came, Militia Rifles to march out
towards Dholpore in the afternoon, with the 3rd
Europeans. On seeing this, I went over to the

Chief Commissioner, to ask whether he would like me to go out with them, or not.*   He desired me to stay in the Fort.   As I left Colonel Fraser a serjeant stepped up, saluted and said, ' Our camp is attacked.'   Guns were heard, I went up to the ramparts, saw two of the enemy's tumbrils explode; then a line of dust as our cavalry and artillery charged and pursued the flying enemy."

I put down my journal here to describe more fully the events of the day.   Soon the wounded began to come in.   The hospital clothes which Mrs. Raikes (at Dr. Farquhar's request) had prepared, were most valuable; indeed, as Colonel Fraser said, they could not have provided for the wounded without the Civil Hospital clothing made up by Mrs. Raikes, and the ladies of Agra.†

Bleeding, lacerated, burnt and contused, the sufferers were carried into the " Motee Musjid," or Pearl Mosque.   In this " Marble Temple," the most graceful building in Asia, rough wooden cots were hastily prepared, the mattrasses, pillows and quilts, which the ladies in the Agra Fort had so long been making, were soon in full demand. Here, covered with wounds, many of which seemed mortal, was carried the gallant Captain Jones ‡, of

---

* I belonged not to the Militia, but to a Rifle Company for the defence of the Fort.

† The Government gave the cloth, and the ladies made up the various articles of hospital clothing.   They were intended for the Civil Hospital in the event of a siege, which happily never took place.

‡ He recovered with the loss of an eye.

Her Majesty's 9th Lancers. Younghusband [*] too came in, surrounded by his faithful Sikh soldiers, who had dragged him out of the well into which he, horse and all, with two or three men on the top of him, had fallen, whilst pursuing the flying Sepoys. Ere long the spacious corridors were filled with sick and wounded men. Dr. Farquhar requested Mrs. Raikes to preside over the hospital arrangements. Of her labours, and of those of many ladies who, with her, soothed and tended the sufferers, I will say not another word. But, I must describe the conduct of the British soldier in the day of sickness and pain. For weeks that the ladies [†] watched over their charge, never was a word said by a soldier which could shock the gentlest ear. When all was over, and when such of the sick and wounded as recovered were declared convalescent, the soldiers, in order, as they expressed it, to show their gratitude for the kindness of the ladies, modestly asked permission to invite their nurses and all the gentry and society of Agra to an entertainment in the beautiful gardens of the Taj. There, under the walls of the marble mausoleum,

---

[*] Lieut. Younghusband would not stay to be cured, but went in with Col. Greathed, and was killed when with Sir Colin Campbell, in the advance on Furuckabad.

[†] The ladies were divided into watches, and attended day and night. To avoid teasing the men by too much nursing, they were in a small separate room, and, *at stated periods*, went round to give tea, jelly, soda water, coffee, soup, or to help in dressing the wounds of the patients. All was done under the orders of the medical officers.

amidst flowers and music, these rough veterans, all
scarred and mutilated as they were, stood up to
thank their countrywomen who had clothed, fed,
and visited them, when they were sick.   Every
lady in Agra was ready to join in this good work,
and not one of them but will bear testimony to the
delicacy of feeling and conduct, as well as the
hearty gratitude, of these brave men.

To return to our immediate subject.   The enemy
who had surprised* our camp were thoroughly
routed.   Greathed began the attack; Cotton, the
superior officer at Agra, took up and furiously
pushed on the pursuit.   The camp, guns, ammunition, and stores fell into our hands.   I return to
my journal.

"Evening.—Our men coming slowly in, quite
done up.   To relieve them we are to furnish guards
to-night.

"*Sunday*, 11*th*.—Last night I mounted guard at
the Umur Singh Gate.   I was elected sergeant;
Money†, corporal; Hugo James, and Wylly (Judge

---

* The surprise happened thus. The civil authorities, on the
9th October, urged Greathed to come in, as the reconnoitring
party sent towards the enemy had been fired at and driven into
Agra. But, on the morning of the 10th, the Magistrate and
other Government officials assured Col. Greathed (as it had
been reported to them) that the enemy had fallen back. *Hinc
illæ lacrymæ.*

† Mr. Wigram Elliott Money, Commissioner of Customs for
the North-Western Provinces. With much spirit he joined
Mr. Harvey, the Commissioner of Agra, who, with a small
party of Englishmen, penetrated nearly up to Delhi early in

of Agra) amongst my men. Thanksgiving for
our victory offered in Church in the Marble Hall.
Well may we be thankful! We had been shut up
in this Fort of Agra since 5th July, and the enemy,
always at hand, never made up their mind to attack us until a couple of hours after a strong column
had marched into the place. We have taken their
camp, treasure, thirteen guns, including one pro-
digious brass piece, and slaughtered heaps of the
mutineers.

"*Friday*, 16*th.*—Re-writing memorandum on the
Police, for the local Government.

" *Tuesday*, 20*th.*—Our Court had lately been
sitting in the Fort. We have now taken rooms
in the Custom House, and carry on work there.

"*Friday*, 23*rd.*—I have been appointed Special
Commissioner under Section 7, Act XIV., of
1857, with authority to issue commissions under
Section 2, Act XVII., with powers of life and
death. John Lawrence writes from Lahore, 21st
October:—'I assure you, when I look back on the
events of the last four months, I am lost in astonishment that any of us are alive. But for the
mercy of God we must have been ruined.

" 'Had the Sikhs joined against us, nothing, hu-
manly speaking, could have saved us. No man
could have hoped, much less foreseen, that they
would have withstood the temptation to avenge
their loss of national independence.

June. Mr. Money's genial presence, on his return, rendered
the Fort of Agra a very tolerable abode to his friends.

" 'Even as matters now are it will be no ordinary task reconstructing the Administration, putting all things straight, getting rid of old abuses, avoiding former mistakes.

" 'I often think and lament over the sad fate, the premature death, of George Christian,' &c. &c.

"There is only one opinion amongst us all here, and this I find was entirely shared by the officers from Delhi, that we owe our preservation, under God's blessing, to John Lawrence and Robert Montgomery, who strained every nerve, not only resolutely to keep order in the Punjab, but also to hurl every available soldier, European, or Sikh, against Delhi."

CHAP. VIII.

A VISIT TO DELHI AFTER THE SIEGE.

DURING the past nine months our four younger children had been with their Governess in the mountains at Landour. Some kind friends escorted them in safety to Agra, where they arrived on 23rd November. On the afternoon of that day, a few hours after our party had passed, a large body of mutineers, in arms, crossed the road by which they had been travelling. These men, the remnant of a mutinous army from Joudpore, had been beaten by our column under the late Colonel Gerard, at Narnol, in the Rewarree country, south-west of Delhi, and then had cut across the Jumna, some two thousand strong, with so much secrecy and despatch, that none of the authorities at Agra knew of their movements until they were actually across the road between Allygurh and Agra.

On the 15th December, finding the road to Cawnpore closed, I determined to take my family home viâ Bombay, passing through Delhi, Umballa, and Ferozpore, and thence proceeding in a country boat down the Indus to Kurachee.

I took a light camp equipage, and arranged to travel hastily through the disturbed districts by post, and from Delhi to make double marches, using my own horses and carriages. I took advantage of Brigadier Seaton's advance from Delhi towards Mynpoorie to hasten up in the wake of his force, and on the 16th, at dusk, we all reached Delhi in safety.

To return to my Journal:—

" *December* 17*th.* — Last night we slept in the old King's bed-room, after dining in what was his Zenana. This morning I went with Saunders to see the breach, the several points of attack and defence, and the posts we held during the memorable days of the siege. The ruined buildings, the trees cut and shorn of their boughs, the fragments of scattered shot and shell, all tell of the intense strife and rage of the conflict.

" During the day I spent an hour in the Marble Hall of Justice, where Brigadier Chamberlain was presiding over a Military Court assembled for the trial of the Nawab of Jhujar. At the commencement of the outbreak, instead of aiding the British officers, he treated them with contempt, lending a rupee to one and a grass-cutter's pony to another; whereas his ancestors had been raised to power by Lord Lake, and enjoyed a large territory from the British Government, on the express condition of aiding us with some four hundred horse. All his men joined the rebel army, his Fort was found fully stored with munitions of war, his Vakeels attended the rebel King of Delhi, &c., &c. After hearing his defence, it seems to me that he has behaved very badly and deserves punishment.

"In the evening we went again over the breach with Brigadier Chamberlain.

"*December* 18*th.*—We went to see the Jumma Musjid, which is held now by a battalion of Beloochees. I sincerely hope that the plan proposed by Mr. Philip Egerton, the Magistrate of Delhi, may be carried out.* He suggests that the Mosque be used henceforth as a Christian Church, and on each of the thousand compartments on the marble floor, the name of one of our Christian Martyrs be inscribed. It is the general opinion that it would be madness to restore this noble building to the Mahommedans.

"In the afternoon I had a long and very interesting walk with Major Reid, the hero who, with his noble little Goorkhas, held our advanced post at Hindoo Rao's house, from first to last, throughout the siege of Delhi. The courage, fortitude and devotion of these officers and men are beyond praise. The Goorkhas under Major Reid were the first natives to throw boldly their lot into ours, and to fight, Brahmin against Brahmin, Hindoo against Hindoo, on the English side. The anxiety with which these brave little Nepalese † were watched in

* I wrote to Sir John Lawrence, urging him to attend to this proposition; I have not heard the result.

† It is satisfactory to observe that the Nepalese are only formidable when under European training and led by English officers. Jung Bahadoor can make little of them; but men such as Fisher was, and Reid is, can lead Goorkhas anywhere and do any thing with them.

their first encounter was intense. The mutineers
came out of Delhi and advanced towards the
Goorkha post, calling out, ' You will not fire at us,
we are all of one caste, we are your brothers and
friends.' The Goorkhas made no demonstration
until the Sepoys had come close up to them, when
they greeted them with a volley, a cheer, and a
rush, kookree in hand, which put all future ideas
of fraternization out of the question.

" I walked over the ruins of Hindoo Rao's house
with astonishment. How men could have held a
building so battered and riddled with shot and
shell, the very target of the enemy, is a marvel;
yet as the siege progressed, when it was proposed
to remove even the sick and wounded in hospital,
they violently protested against being carried away
from their comrades even to a place of safety.
In this hospital Major Reid pointed out the mark
where a patient had been cut in half by a round
shot. After spending an hour or two on the heights,
where the Major had been engaged in *twenty-five
regular fights*, to say nothing of an incessant cannonade which went on day and night for months,
we proceeded to the spot on the bridge over the
canal in the suburb, where he fell on the morning
of the assault, in his twenty-sixth engagement.
He lost nearly all his little Goorkhas, and can with
difficulty, if at all, replace them. He enlists only
the fighting castes, and wonderful soldiers they
are; the only men in India, so far as I know, who
never drink, loot, nor run away. I had heard that
when their leader was knocked over, the Goorkhas,

unable to advance, and unwilling to retreat, sate down on the bridge under a shower of bullets. This Major Reid denies. He has a terrible gash in his head, and ought to be taken care of by Government, as he is not the sort of man to take care of himself.*

"19*th*. — We drove ten miles out of Delhi to spend the day at the country house of Sir Theophilus Metcalfe, near the Kootub Minar. It was a strange sight — a house full of books, pictures, and elegant furniture — in the middle of the mutineers' camp, or at least of the country overrun by them. I questioned the servants how they had managed to preserve their master's property intact, when not a stone belonging to any Christian was left standing all over the country. They answered evasively. My belief is that the King of Delhi had the place preserved for his own use, and considering the beauty of the house and grounds, he showed his good taste. I may here mention that I read several of the King's orders, written with his own pencil, and proving what an ungrateful old man he is. The English saved his family from the most cruel tyranny of the Mahrattas, gave them back royal rank, and bestowed an ample pension, yet this hoary-headed sinner orders all Christians to be murdered, &c. &c.

---

* I never saw Major Reid before I went to Delhi, and know merely what I have described of him here. I may therefore suggest how *invaluable* his services might be if he were employed to raise 10,000 Goorkhas, for distribution, not into separate corps, but into fifty different regiments, in the mode described in a future chapter.

" Amongst the papers one amused me. It was from a native officer at Meerut, and ran somewhat thus : —

" After compliments the writer informs the Asylum of the Universe that His Majesty's sway from Meerut to Cawnpore is complete. In the district of Bolundshuhr, however, a rebel, one Turnbull, is trying to create a disturbance. 'If your Majesty will send a detachment of your victorious troops, he will easily be put down.'

" ' One Turnbull ' meant Mr. George Turnbull, the former Magistrate and Collector of Bolundshuhr, now Judge of Meerut. He, with Mr. Sapte, exerted himself to maintain order in the country, and thus obtained the distinction of being denounced as a ' rebel ' to the King. Yesterday we all went, a large party of ladies and gentlemen, with Mr. and Mrs. Saunders, to see the King. He is a withered old man of ninety. I found him propped up with cushions on a bed, in a small house which formerly was occupied by a humble follower. I sat down on a chair by his side*, heard him rambling on about his dreams and quoting some verses of his own composition, and then left without addressing him. The ladies saw the Queen ; she was in a very bad humour, and grumbled at having insufficient fuel. The King

---

* As a proof of the sensitive temper of the time, I may mention that I saw an account of this interview in an English newspaper, in which the writer expressed his surprise and disgust that I took off my hat when I entered the house in which the old King was.

G

has ten personal attendants, which seems a full allowance for a man who has only one room to live in.   I have been reading the papers connected with the old King's capture. His life was guaranteed by Hodson, under the authority of General Wilson, *in order to prevent his escape.* Saunders had nothing whatever to do with it.

"In the evening I went out with General Penny on his elephant, to see the side streets of the city. For miles not a creature save a half-starved cat, and here and there an old hag groping about amidst the bones, old papers, and rags with which this once wealthy and populous place is strewed. It is as a city of the dead.

"Saunders * is working here as Commissioner ably and successfully, and as hospitable as ever."

---

* My first acquaintance with Mr. Charles B. Saunders was at Amritsur, in 1852. It was on the occasion of Sir Henry Lawrence's departure from the Punjab. One sample, the first I had, of Mr. Saunders' hospitality, will suffice. He had filled his house and grounds with friends to that degree that he and Mrs. Saunders were living in a tent pitched *on the top of the house,* in very inclement weather. As Deputy Commissioner of Amritsur, Mr. Saunders won all hearts. The old Sikh chiefs really adored him. Driven from Moradabad, where he was Magistrate, early in June, by the mutiny of the 29th N. I., he did excellent service in the country between Kurnal and Delhi, and accompanied our troops in the storm and gradual advance upon that city. Mild yet courageous, gentle yet firm, he has that rare mixed character of decision and suavity which is now beyond all price in India.

CHAP. IX.

FROM Agra to Delhi we had travelled post, as it was considered on all hands imprudent to march with ladies and children on that road. It was a great delight to us all once more to find ourselves sufficiently far from mutineers of all sorts, to be able with a slight escort to avail ourselves of our tents, and we marched with comfort from Delhi to Umballa.

Our friend Mr. Robert Montgomery, the present Chief Commissioner of Oude, arranged to meet us on our journey to Ferozpore, and we were here looking forward to a pleasant voyage down the Indus to Bombay.

At Umballa, however, I received a letter from Mr. Jackson, late officiating Chief Commissioner of Oude, informing me, that having met with a severe accident (a broken leg) on the retreat from Lucknow, he was unable to accompany Sir Colin Campbell further, that His Excellency had written to Colonel Fraser, the Chief Commissioner at Agra, for my services, and had requested him to propose to me to accompany him on his advance from Cawnpore to Furuckabad and Mynpoorie, &c. The duty required was "to superintend the introduction of order, the re-establishment of our Government in the provinces from which Sir Colin had expelled the mutineers, and the punishing the insurgents." It was further notified to me that it was considered of "vital importance to the interests of Government that military successes should be immediately followed by the introduction of an efficient police, &c. &c." As Sir Colin Campbell and Mr. Jackson agreed in thinking it desirable that I should thus attend upon His Excellency, I accepted the invitation, and here subjoin copies of two letters written by me on the 26th and 27th of December, which will explain my proceedings better than any detail I can now give.

" *To Colonel Fraser, C.B., Chief Commissioner at Agra.*

"My dear Fraser,
        " Mr. Money writes me word that Sir C. Campbell had expressed to you, his wish that I should be deputed to his camp.

" I have no letters from you, or from your secretary on the subject, but I think it my duty in these times, to express my readiness to wait upon His Excellency.

" I have not yet formally and officially notified my acceptance of the leave granted me, and you may easily cancel my application.

" Sick and worn out as I am, I still would accompany the army as long as I had a leg to stand upon, and I might be, with God's blessing, of some use to my country. At all events, I cannot neglect such an invitation, and I await here your permission to join the camp at once.

"Write, if you please, to Mr. Saunders at Delhi, and he will telegraph your instructions to me.

" Your's, very sincerely,

" C. RAIKES."

To Sir Colin Campbell I wrote thus:—

" SIR,

" I have this day received a letter from Mr. Jackson, dated 13th December, in which he informs me that your Excellency has applied for my services, to attend your Camp.

" I had heard this from a private friend a day or two ago, and at once wrote to Colonel Fraser to request him to express to you my desire to wait upon you.

" My health is not strong, but I hope that I may be able to arrange such details of the Civil Administration as may be committed to my charge, and that completed, I shall hope to proceed to England with my family.

" I shall feel deeply mortified if Colonel Fraser should object to my accepting the duty for which your Excellency has been pleased to nominate me. It is one of which any Englishman might be proud, and I feel sensible of the honour done to me.

" I have, &c.,

" C. RAIKES.

"Camp, Umballa: 27th December, 1857."

I also wrote to General Mansfield, Chief of the

Staff, to say that if any other civil officer had been deputed, owing to my absence from Agra, I nevertheless claimed the right of serving Sir Colin. Not to quote other letters, I may here give the General's reply. Kind it is and courteous, like every communication which I received from him or Sir Colin:—

"6 A.M., January 3rd, 1858.

"Camp Kurowlie, three miles beyond left bank Kalee Nuddee.

"MY DEAR SIR,

"I have this morning received your letter of the 30th ultimo and shown it to His Excellency. He will be delighted to see you, and has not heard as yet of any deputation of another civilian by the Agra Government.

"Should he do so, nothing will permit interference with the arrangement respecting yourself, proposed for your consideration through Mr. Jackson.

"The garrison of Futtehgurh tried to defend the suspension bridge over the Kalee Nuddee, or rather attacked our working party employed in the repair of it, and compelled us to engage them. They lost all their guns and a few hundred men killed. Our loss was trifling.

"We advance close up to Futtehgurh to-day.

"I am, &c.,

"W. MANSFIELD."

Pending a reply to my letters to Agra and the Head-quarters Camp, I paid a visit to the Maharaja of Putialee. This powerful Chief had rendered such important services to the British

Government during the campaign against the mutineers at Delhi, that I was anxious, on behalf of the Agra Government, to express my acknowledgments. After a visit of some days to Putialee, I can more than ever enter into the feelings of aversion with which our ablest officers regard any further annexation of native States. I can conceive no greater crime, nor any more extravagant political blunder, than it would be to annex such a principality as this of Putialee. To say that the subjects of this State are as contented and happy as those in our own conterminous districts is not enough. They get, I believe, cheaper and speedier justice than their near neighbours at Paniput did under the late Agra régime. They are, if anything, better fed, clothed, and housed than our own subjects; and, what is no small matter, they are, so long as we leave them alone, *on our side.* In order to cement the existing good feeling between us and native independent or protected States, we might well assure them, for the future, that even in the event of a failure of direct heirs, we have no wish to assume charge of new territories. Our true strength is in the support and confidence of our native allies, not in any further increase of territory.

The Maharaja received me with great ceremony and splendour, and lodged all our party in the Motee Bagh, or Pearl Garden, a country residence, or rather a painted hall, surrounded by flowers and fountains. Here, leading me aside, he gave earnest warning of the dangers of too large a Sikh army.

"Wait, sir," said he, "until this excitement of victory, this surfeit of plunder, be over; wait till you mass large bodies of Sikhs in your cantonments, and then remember that I warned you of the danger." This conversation made the greater impression on me as confirming the views of Brigadier Chamberlain, who a few days before had said to me, "The Sepoys have waited a hundred years to mutiny, the Sikhs, if subject to like temptations, will not wait ten!" He also had received from the Raja of Jheend a similar warning. Making full allowance for the hereditary prejudice which these Rajahs, as Malwa* Sikhs, have against the Manjha† Sikhs, I yet consider that we must be careful how we handle our Sikh levies; but I shall return to this subject in a future chapter.

Mr. Douglas Forsyth, now Secretary to the Chief Commissioner of Oude, was, at the time of my visit to Umballa, the Deputy Commissioner of that District. From all that Mr. Forsyth told me, it appears perfectly certain that the Maharaja‡ assisted us most materially and zealously during the late troubles, and indeed it is not too much to say, that without his help the Umballa Cantonment would

---

* On the left bank of the Sutlej River.

† Between the Beas and Ravee, about Amritsur, &c.

‡ The Maharaja, though very manly and straightforward in his manners, is not free from some of the conceits of Asiatic diplomacy. "Tell me," said he quietly to Mr. Forsyth, "whether Mr. Raikes is sent here to criticise my conduct; I have done much to show my respect and to make him welcome; but if he wants to find fault with me I will try to do even more."

hardly have been preserved. At the end of May, or early in June, when summoned to the station, he came clad in a suit of mail, driving his own elephant like a true Indian warrior, and spared neither personal fatigue nor exertion to prove his zeal for the British Government and against the mutineers. I have before me a newspaper,* lithographed by the rebels during the time that our troops were before Delhi, and dated to correspond with our 23rd August, 1857. To give a brief extract of one of the leading articles will suffice:—

" PUNJAB.—Although it appears, by the report of travellers from Lahore, that the murder and destruction of the impure infidels has taken place, yet some eye-witnesses declare that they hold forts and may be seen moving about during the day-time, and in short they have not been so thoroughly swept away as, by the favour of God, has been the case to the eastward. Still there is not a question that the Government of the infidels is over in the Punjab and elsewhere. But they receive supplies from the Maharaja of Putialee, who above all ungrateful men, assists and supports them. Therefore, a force should be sent out against him," &c. &c.

Soon after our return from Putialee, orders came for me to join the army in the field; so I prepared at once to retrace my steps to Agra, and thence to proceed to Head-quarters at Furuckabad.

* This paper was taken when our troops entered the Palace at Delhi.

CHAP. X.

FROM UMBALLA TO SIR COLIN CAMPBELL'S CAMP AT FURUCKABAD.

ON my return from Umballa towards Delhi and Furuckabad, I paid a visit to the Nawab at Kurnal. This man, whose house and land is on the high road between Umballa and Delhi, had very early to make up his mind either to join the chiefs around Delhi, who had forsaken their allegiance to the British Government, or to take his stand with us.

Mr. Le Bas, the Judge of Delhi, after undergoing the greatest peril, escaped from that city to Kurnal. Soon after his arrival, during the interval that preceded the advance of our troops from Umballa viâ Kurnal, and just as the defection became known, when we had no military force near Kurnal, and all men watched anxiously the conduct of each local chief, the Nawab of Kurnal came to Mr. Le Bas and addressed him to the following effect.

" Sir, I have spent a sleepless night in meditating on the state of affairs : I have decided to throw in my lot with yours. My sword, my purse, and my followers are at your disposal."

So well did he act up to the engagement thus made, that after the fall of Delhi a testimonial was

put into his hand by Mr. Le Bas, equally honourable
to both. As a mark of regard the Judge gave the
Nawab his favourite horse*, and a letter of thanks
for his public services.

Amongst other marks of devotion to our cause,
the Nawab had raised a troop of one hundred horse,
armed and equipped on the model of the Punjab
Mounted Police Corps. I can speak for their efficiency, as some of these men escorted me, under a
native officer connected with the Nawab, from
Kurnal to Benares.

I consider the conduct of this Mahomedan noble-
man to deserve special commendation, and I
trust that he has received suitable reward. Other
Mahomedan Talookdars no doubt professed loyalty,
and in some instances did good service, but few so
entirely identified themselves with the cause which
in May 1857, was generally considered by the people the losing one. Many who have received great
credit for loyalty, were mere watchers of the event
—as polite to the mutineers as to us, or as the
natives expressed it, "*keeping their feet in both
stirrups.*" My old friend at Kurnal was an honourable exception, he made no sort of parade of his
services, and his only complaint when I saw him
was, that we were far too gentle and generous to

* An animal of rare beauty and value, whose speed had
saved his master's life in the flight from Delhi. I have these
particulars from the Nawab, as I am not personally acquainted
with Mr. Le Bas. But as I saw that gentleman's letters and
the horse, I can trust to the general correctness of the information given me by the Nawab.

rebels in general, and to his own rebellious neighbours in particular.

After leaving my wife and family at Meerut, I
proceeded viâ Agra, to take charge of my new duties
with the Commander in Chief.   At Agra I heard
that the only remaining child of my late son-in-law,
Mr. Christian, had, whilst a captive in the Palace
at Lucknow, sunk under a disease brought on by
bad food and confinement.

From this period up to the end of the month, I
revert to my journal, — amplified as it is by some
few papers which are inserted in order to throw
light on the occurrences of the period.

" *Wednesday*, 13*th*. — Busy day at Agra. I went
to speak to Dr. Farquhar.*

" All I could extort from him was, that he believed I was acting from a sense of duty, and so
far right.

" *Thursday*, 14*th*. — Bought   tents,   brace   of
double-barrelled pistols, two horses.   Hartigan†
got me a first-rate Arab charger, when I was in
despair of finding a good horse.

" Colonel Fraser wishes me to wait to go to the

---

* He had written to me thus on the 5th — " But a more important, because a public, consideration is, are you right in
occupying such a post, with a shattered body ; for, by all
accounts, your duties will be more physical than mental.   I
heartily sympathise with your desire to serve, for I have applied
to join the Field Hospital as soon as I am relieved here ; but I
should think I did wrong if I had not at present a *mens sana
in corpore sano.*"

† The sergeant of the 9th Lancers who made the speech
about the lady nurses in the Taj.

Chief with a detachment of the Queen's 38th Foot here from Mynpoorie. I can't wait, and have ordered a relay of mail horses to be ready to take me to Mynpoorie, thence I must ride into camp with any escort I can get. Captain Bruce, who has just come in from head-quarters, has kindly lent me his tent there until my things come up.

" *Sunday*, 17*th*. — Head-Quarters Camp, Futty-gurh. I have had time to look about me. I started on Friday morning with Mr. Fullerton* in my travelling carriage. The first horse broke the shafts; however, we patched up the carriage and pushed on. The Mynpoorie folk seemed very glad to see me, and at Shekoabad and Ghurwur brought out some of the old 'ryklas' which they have been using against the mutineers, to fire a salute in my honour. What with their salutations and the complaints of ' *be-duk-ilee*† ' it was late before we reached Mynpoorie. We found the Magistrate, Mr. Boldero; my friend Chase his assistant, and the rest of the Civil Staff of the district, taking their supper in the old Sepoy guard-room attached to the Cutcherry ‡ ; the Cutcherry itself being a

---

* The Reverend Mr. Fullerton is the devoted and excellent missionary of the American Presbyterian Mission at Agra. He went to gather his scattered flock at Furuckabad.

† Be-duk-ilee means dispossession. Thousands were forcibly dispossessed during the mutiny, and came praying for restitution the moment we resumed sway in our rural districts.

‡ Court house, in which the Magistrate-Collector transacts business, and the repository of the public records of the district.

heap of ruins, like every other English building in the place, the Church only excepted.*

" In the morning I received crowds of old friends, each anxious to declare his delight at having the 'sahib log' (gentlemen) back again. Balances of revenue coming in well. Sepoys in hiding in sugar cane fields all over the country, and abused by everybody.

" I took a melancholy walk over the station once so dear to me; saw my old house in ruins, the garden and lawn overgrown, tangled, and out of order; the Church-yard defaced, my serai lately used as a barrack for the rebel Rajah. Rao Bowannie Singh came to pay his respects: very civil, but I suspect him, and at best consider him but as a fair-weather friend.

" We drove to Bhowgong†, where, as the people knew I was coming, there was a great demonstration of loyalty. My poor Jemadar Balkishun had been killed here by the mutineers in May or June. I went into the Tuhseelee, one of the last public buildings constructed by me in 1852, before I left Mynpoorie for Lahore. The place had been occupied since July as a barrack by the rebel Rajah. Under the gateway were the scribblings of the mutineers on the wall—caricatures of the English,

---

* It is a curious fact that at Agra, Allygurh, Mynpoorie, Futtygurh, and other places, less damage was done to the Churches than to the private dwellings of the English.

† A large town, full of ill-conditioned Mahomedans, on the grand trunk-road, at the junction of the high-road to Agra *via* Mynpoorie.

with appropriate mottos, such as ' *Maro Furingee*,'
' *Furingee rota nye*,'* were scratched over the place.
The Tehsildar of Bhowgong, who I presume had
not noticed these hieroglyphics, looked very much
ashamed when I suggested the expediency of a
little whitewash. As I passed through the obse-
quious crowd outside (knowing the character of the
people of this town), I could not help reflecting
how different would have been my reception if
Wilson at Delhi, and Sir Colin at Cawnpore and
Furuckabad, had not vindicated the honour of our
nation.

" At Bewur we mounted horses which the kindness of our friends at Mynpoorie had provided,
and with an escort of five and twenty Mynpoorie
Sowars pushed on towards Futtygurh. The sun
was fast sinking as we approached within sight of
the head-quarters camp.

" Sir Colin (who had just returned from an expedition to Walpole's brigade, which was watching
the Ghat on the Ramfunga river, about ten miles
from our camp across the Ganges in an easterly
direction), received me with the utmost cordiality
and kindness. I dined with him last night, meet-
ing Sir David Baird, Lord Seymour, the two
Alisons (one minus an arm), Major Metcalfe,
Colonel Stirling, &c. &c.

" This morning I breakfasted with the Chief, and
have since been to the staff mess tent to Church,

* Down with the English — the English are crying.

where the Rev. Mr. Mackie preached an excellent sermon.

" *Monday*, 18*th*. — I made the following note from information given me by an Italian gentleman, who has lately escaped from Lucknow.

" Mr. Steven Reghelini, a Catholic of Sirdhano, son of Major R. of the Begum Sumroo's service, a British pensioner of 200 rupees per mensem, went to Lucknow in search of some employment, and was in the city opposite the iron bridge living in a hired house, when the mutineers attacked Lucknow. He was protected, with Mr. Browne and several others, by Mirza Hatim Ali Beg, late Moonsiff of Chunar, and his son Sukawut Ali Beg, Mr. Gubbins's Moonshee, the last man to stay in the Residency, and who left with Mr. Gubbins's permission on the 30th of June. Mrs. Beale, wife of the Second Master of the Bareilly College, was one of the party saved by Sukawut Ali and his father. Mr. Reghelini relates of Lucknow thus:—

" ' *Lucknow.*

" ' Meerza Birjis Kudr Buhadoor is Sooba (or Viceroy) of Oude, under the King of Delhi, about twelve or thirteen years old. His mother is Huzrat Muhl. This boy is son of Wajid Ali Shah, the King of Oude, now prisoner in Calcutta.

" ' Prime Minister Shurfoodowla, once Naib at Lucknow.

" ' Momoo Khan, at Kaisar Bagh, Daroga of Dewan Khana Khanja.

" ' Mujuffer Ali Khan, General, nephew of Shurfoodowla.

" ' Ruhmut Oolla, Head Moonshee of Shurfoodowla.

" ' Ahmud Ali, or Chota Mia, has charge of the magazine.

" ' Maharaj Balkissan, Dewan.

" ' Unwur Jee, Darogah of Vuzeer's Dewan Khana.

" ' Ali Riza Beg, Kotwal, formerly Extra Assistant of Dureabad, under the British Government.

" ' Ahmed Oolla Shah, Mahomedan leader, who came with the mutineers from Fyzabad. He was released from gaol; a regular rebel; was once in gaol in Agra. Through his example the troops take courage in the day of battle; he has been twice wounded.

" ' *Artillery.*

" ' Fyzabad Horse Artillery, six 6-pounders.

" ' Colonel Gunge   Ditto   Ditto.

" ' Nusseerabad   Ditto nine guns.

" ' A made up new battery, six guns.

" ' Some guns left at Chinhut by Sir H. Lawrence; one large elephant gun.

" ' Muchie Bowun guns, left by the British; two large rusty 24-pounders.

" ' *Cavalry.*

| " ' 300 Sowars. | 15th Irregulars. |
| " ' 300 Ditto. | 15th Recruits. |

H

" ' 400 Sowars,   12th. — Fight well, Hur-
                              riana Ranghurs.

" ' 500 Ditto, under Moulvee Mustan Khan.

" ' 500 Ditto, under Sheikh Sookum.

" ' 300 Ditto, late Captain Daly's.

" ' A few of Hardinge's Russala.

" ' About 2000 troopers, Soobah's new levies,
not well armed, badly mounted.

" ' *Infantry.*

" ' 1 Bohl ha pultun, from Fyzabad.

" ' 1 Bullum teer. (Volunteers.)

" ' 12 Police battalions.

" ' Some sappers and miners.

" ' 50 Regiments Nujeeb, some 100, some 200,
in all about 10,000 men.

" ' 4000 Infantry Nusseerabad camp, from Delhi.

" ' *Petty Princes.*

" ' Raja Man Singh, with followers.

" '   „   Goorbucs Singh.

" '   „   Nawab Ali Khan.

" '   „   Benee Mallkoo.

" '   „   Lal Madhoo, of Kala Konkar.

" ' Chowdree Hushmut Ali, of Sundeela.

" ' Munsub Ali, of Russoolabad.

" ' In all about 200,000 men in arms in Lucknow
alone.'

" Hodson came in from the Ram Gunga, where his
horse are encamped with Walpole. He came, by
order of Sir Colin, to inform me that certain Ma-

homedans in the vicinity of his camp had offered
to assist, making no conditions for themselves
whatever, and saying, that if any fault should hereafter be proved against them, they asked for no
consideration ; might he, asked Hodson, under the
circumstances use them ? I said, if these men offer
without any condition to assist you, I can have no
objection, and if you will send in their names and
abode, I will tell you how far you may trust
them.

" *Tuesday*, 19*th*.—Rode early to the City, Palace
and Payeen Bagh; ordered up heaps of the rebel
Duftur (record office), to be examined at leisure. I
received letters from Government (Agra) with important communications as to the condition of the
Meerut Division with respect to the Rohilcund
insurgents. I took these papers over to Sir Colin,
who very frankly stated his views to me, and pro-
mised to send on the documents with some pressing
letters from the Magistrate of Etawah to Lord
Canning.

" In addition to the public papers mentioned
above, I placed before His Excellency the following
private memorandum, written by one of the ablest
Civil officers in the North Western Provinces,
whose intimate knowledge of Rohilcund stamped
value on every word : —

" ' 1. The Bijnore rebels are getting troublesome
and bold. Small parties have crossed the Ganges;
and, within the last few days, a larger body of 500
or 600 men — some say more — crossed, and burnt

the Thaneh at Meeranpoor, in the south-east corner
of the Moozufurnuggur district. They recrossed on
our cavalry appearing. But the presence of 4000
or 5000 rebels, with guns, on the east bank of the
Ganges, who are constantly threatening invasion,
and are, doubtless, trying to stir up the disaffected
against Government, has a bad effect on the district. Our troops are harassed with the duty of
watching these rebels, and cannot do it effectually;
and the sooner a column moves across and destroys
the Bijnore rebels the better; for a slight mistake
on our part, or a chance bit of success on theirs,
might enable them to disturb the peace of the
whole division to an extent that, with the few
troops left here, would give serious trouble.

"'2. Further down the Ganges, opposite Anoop-
shahur, large parties of rebels are constantly
threatening to cross, and firing on our people.
They keep the district officers and all the troops
constantly watching the bank of the river. The
fact that, above and below, this occurs without
any attempt to punish the rebels, is, to the people,
proof of weakness.

"'3. It is well known that no reinforcements
have reached this, and that troops have gone, and
still continue to go—mounted and foot police are
still constantly moving down—*from* this, and do
not return; and the well wishers of Government
on the east of the Ganges, who are earnestly begging for the advance of Government troops, report
that the evil disposed on this side, are continually
informing their friends, the rebels in Rohilcund,

that no troops are left here, and inviting them to come over, and assuring them, if they will come, thousands and thousands will join them.

" ' 4. This is all talk, of course ; but still it is talk that should be put a stop to without delay. The Nawab of Rampoor, who knows all that is going on in Rohilcund, has applied for the loan of eight 6-pounder guns, with ammunition, to enable him to resist the attacks which he declares will be made upon him if the reoccupation of Rohilcund is longer delayed.

" ' 5. This requisition, strongly seconded by the Commissioner of Rohilcund, has been submitted to the General of the Division, who cannot comply with it.

" ' 6. The Nawab—who has behaved in a most admirable manner—fears that, strengthened by the numbers of rebels driven from Oude by fear, and from Futtehgurh by our advance to that place, the Bareilly rebels will push up towards him. The inability to comply with his request for guns, and the non-appearance of any signs of an advance from this side, will greatly discourage him and all the well-wishers of Government, who, in the event of an influx of rebels and mutineers from the south-east, without any support from the west, will be exposed to great danger. If the rebels find the Upper Doab is not reinforced, their threats and attempts to cross will probably be matured into a serious combination with the smouldering dis-affection, which has been suppressed but not eradi-cated.

" ' 7. In the meantime, the unfortunate Hindoos are being oppressed and plundered. A large amount of revenue is being exacted, which it would be hard to demand again from the people, who have been withholding it as long as they could, and begging for assistance ; and while the revenue, already nearly all collected in the Upper Doab, is being rapidly expended, nearly fifty lacs of rupees, which might be got within the next three months in Rohilcund, and with which nearly all financial difficulties would disappear, are locked up when most urgently wanted.

" ' 8. Strong reasons in favour of an advance into Rohilcund from the west and north-west are indicated above.

" ' 9. With the exception of the rebels collected on the banks of the Ganges near Bijnore and Anoop-shahur, who would be disposed of by columns of very moderate strength, there would be no opposition till the troops concentrated near Bareilly,—if then. The greater part of the Bijnore and Moradabad districts have been kept in order by the Nawab of Rampoor, who has his own people now at his beck. The force advancing from the north-west might be joined by 1000 Goorkhas, with four guns, now impatiently waiting at Huldewanee, below Nynee Tal, for permission to clear their front.

" ' 10. To the south and east of Bareilly, thousands upon thousands of Rajpoots are waiting, eager to take revenge for the oppression they have suffered for the last eight months, and to cut off all fugitives attempting to escape that way.

" '11. Every day the Rohilcund rebels near the Ganges are getting bolder, and the necessity for a speedy advance of troops to go into that province from the north-west side is becoming more urgent.'

" 'Meerut : January 9th, 1858.'

" *Wednesday, 20th.*—An ordinary man might be perplexed at the confusion of interests and circumstances which invite Sir Colin's attention just now. The local Government at Agra, urging an immediate advance on Bareilly, and giving amongst other reasons the following : —

" The left bank of the Ganges, from the mountains right down to Sir Colin's front, swarming with Sepoys and Mahomedan rebels, with cavalry, infantry and artillery, continually threatening to cross the river, which is fordable at the present season; every now and then making a hasty rush across, swooping down to cut up some unfortunate outlying Police or Tehseel (revenue collection) station, to carry off if possible some luckless European telegraph signaller or patrol, and then recrossing the river to laugh at our beards. On the other hand come letters from the highest functionaries of State in Calcutta and elsewhere, pointing out the necessity of an immediate move upon Lucknow. The considerations which recommend both the advance upon Bareilly and the destruction of Lucknow, are momentous; in short it is obviously desirable and necessary to attack the enemy in both directions ere long, and, if possible,

H 4

in both directions *at once;* but where are the troops
to come from? No force that Sir Colin can collect
will be more than enough to smash Lucknow, with
its seven miles of buildings, two hundred thousand
fighting men, as many more armed citizens, its
powerful defences, artillery, &c. Sir Colin has
represented to the Governor-General his own
views, and now quietly awaits, like a true soldier,
any orders that may be given.

" *22nd.* — The citizens affected to desire to illu-
minate Furuckabad, in honour of Sir Colin's occupation of the district. I say no; you have had
too many English men and women murdered
here; but if you wish to show your loyalty, let me
see you support the British Government in every
way by your conduct and influence. An attempt
made to open communication with me by the rebel
Queen at Lucknow.

" I brought to His Excellency's notice that the
enemy had recrossed the Ganges, not twenty miles
hence on our flank, and driven away our Police
Thanah at Kaemgunge, and urged that he should
give the civil power support; the Chief makes
no promises.

" *23rd.* — I submitted for the consideration of
the Commander-in-Chief this memorandum: —

" ' One thousand rebels have crossed at Sooruj-
poer Ghat, opposite Kumpil. Nine thousand horse
and foot, with nine guns, are preparing to cross,
and getting a bridge ready.

" ' They are said to be led by Mooltan Khan, of
Mhow, near Kaemgunge. This is the report of a

Jemadar, located at Kumpil, by Captain Brad-
ford.'

" I also wrote to the Foreign Secretary with the
Governor-General, informing him that certain
Oude Chiefs wished to open a communication with
me, but that I could do nothing in the matter
without the Governor-General's permission.

" *Sunday*, 24*th*. — Sent in the following memorandum to Sir Colin: —

" ' Peera Hurkaruh, employed by Mahomed Us-
kuree and Mahomed Mohsun, left Lucknow on
Monday, 18th current (one day later than the last
messenger to Hurdeo Bux), and reports as follows:

" ' The Begum (mother of the present King of
Oude) had just held a Durbar, on which occasion
she summoned all the native commandants of
troops and the rebel Chiefs, and told them that she
was unable to keep them in the pay of the King any
longer, and that she desired to pay them up, and
discharge them.

" ' The soldiers and rebels replied that in a day
or two they would attack the British force near
Alumbagh, and either drive the British out of the
place, or perish in the attempt.

" ' A general attack upon General Outram's position is expected.

" 'But a letter from Sheikh Fuzl Kureem informs
us that the Oude Chukladars and provincial Chiefs,
Nazims, &c., hearing of the advance of British
troops towards Oude, will make no revenue payments to the nominal King at Lucknow, and that

although the Begum and her Minister, Shurfoodowla, have urged the troops to guard the ferries,
and to press the Nazims for payment, they (the
soldiers) refuse to leave Lucknow; so he argues it
is very doubtful whether they will keep their promise of attacking the British force.

" ' Nana Sahib is absent from his camp; has left
his tents with about one hundred men, at Mulaon;
is either in his Zenana at Biroa, or gone to Rhy-
rabad.

" ' The Chukladar of Tundyaon with Dul Singh
and other Talookdars, seven thousand men and
six guns, is moving towards Newra Ghat on the
Ganges.   (This is nearly opposite Kanouj.)'

" *Monday, 25th.* — Rode to the city; I spoke to
the Commander-in-Chief about the Kaemgunge
rebels, and gave him the following note on the
subject : —

" ' From several reports from Kumpil and Shum-
sabad, I gather that a considerable rebel force of
cavalry and zemindarry levies of matchlock men,
with several guns, some say nine, some say twelve,
are moving towards Furuckabad, and intend to
halt to-day at Bunourie, which is three coss from
the Mhow gate of the city.

" ' They give out that they intend to attack the
city, &c. &c., and to fight.

" ' They are doubtless encouraged by the bad
characters in the city, whom it has not been
easy for the Magistrate to identify or to expel
hitherto.

" ' These men might get over the city wall, and

plunder and do mischief, and the Magistrate has no sufficient force as yet to prevent them.'

" *Tuesday*, 26*th*. — Rode to the city, saw in the Kotwallie (police station) the bodies of two of the Nawabs who had been implicated in the murders and robberies of our poor countrymen at Futtey-gurh. They had just been hanged by order of the Magistrate. I rode over to see their houses, and notwithstanding my indignation at the conduct of the Nawabs of Furuckabad, the sight was a sad one. A fine palace full of every luxurious appliance, mirrors, chandeliers, lustres, pictures, books, and furniture, suddenly deserted — not a human creature left — save one or two withered hags, in the Zenana; cats, parrots, pet dogs, clamorous for food. Outside, in the shady terraces and summer houses, and round the family mausoleum, wandered animals in quest of water or food, nylghai*, bara-singha (twelve-horned deer), and other pet deer; on the wall a little black puppy yelping, and a dog howling piteously; in the poultry yard geese shut up, and making a frightful noise; at the stables grain for seven horses ready steeped and in separate portions, but the horses pawing, looking round, and starving, with food in their sight; monkeys, cockatoos, and an elephant, who had broken loose, and was helping himself to food — formed one of the strangest yet saddest pictures I ever saw. I took care that the animals were fed. As for the princes who so lately were masters of all this luxury, nobody had ventured even to claim their bodies,

* Blue-deer.

and it remained for strangers to give them decent sepulture.

" It seems but the other day that I, then Magistrate of Furuckabad, breakfasted in this very garden house with some of the family who, though receiving princely fortunes at our hands, have now been so ready to slay and spoil their benefactors! How odious is every scene here, once so pleasing to me.

" As I know that the rebels are coming down upon us, I have been round the city outside, from the Mhow Gate. The walls are good for nothing, and it is useless trying to repair them.

" On my return home, I was reading my letters, when Sir Colin came up to my tent, and told me the details of the force which Sir John Lawrence was sending down to Umballa to operate on Rohilcund. He then went on to the next tent to call upon Sir A. Wilson, who has just joined the Camp to command the Artillery.

" At noon General Mansfield called, and told me that a brigade would march at ten this evening to disperse the rascals at Shumshabad, &c. In the afternoon General Grant and Hodson called. The latter remarked to me that his Sikhs are anxiously watching our treatment of mutineers. They say, ' Just now you are very angry with the Sepoys, but six months hence the Lord Sahib (Governor-General) will pardon them all.' Hodson is clearly of opinion, that unless the mutineers are fairly hunted down and sentenced either to death or transportation for life, that we may expect before long a Sikh mutiny. They are watching to see whether mutiny is not condoned by the British Government, and if it is condoned the Sikhs will have their turn; for they will argue, 'If we get the best of it we gain every thing, and if we lose we shall be as well off as we were before.' These are the natural speculations of semi-barbarous men.

"At night I warned Mr. Power* for duty, to go out with the brigade. I found it difficult to convince him that two thousand men, quietly slumbering around, would in the course of half-an-hour be under arms, and on the march to attack the enemy. Scarce a creature in the camp, save General Mansfield, Brigadier Adrian Hope, Hodson and I, knew the plans of the Commander-in-Chief. The men had gone to bed as usual, when quietly orders were issued, and by half-past ten Adrian Hope, with his brigade †, was on his march through Furuckabad to attack the enemy, who were encamped some twelve miles from the city near Shumshabad.

"*Wednesday*, 27*th*.—Golab Rai Duffadar, of Hodson's Horse, arrived at my tent this evening. He states, thus: ' On arriving at Roshunabad at daybreak, Captain Hodson ascertained that the enemy were encamped in force at Shumshabad. A body of their cavalry, about four hundred in number, were

---

* Mr. John Power was Magistrate of Furuckabad. It was he who so gallantly held Mynpoorie with Major Raikes, throughout June 1857, in spite of the mutiny and desertion of the Sepoys there stationed.

† Two squadrons 9th Lancers, 200 Hodson's Horse, one troop and one battery Bengal Artillery, 43rd Royal Highlanders, 53rd Regiment, 4th Punjab Rifles.

preparing to charge our cavalry. Hodson went at them with his Horse; they ran, leaving four guns. Hodson pursued for two miles; twenty-five or thirty of the enemy stood, fought, and were cut to pieces. Our artillery blew up one of the enemy's ammunition waggons. I saw five or six of Hodson's Horse *hors de combat.* I saw no European private soldiers killed. Captain McDouall* is badly wounded. Hodson has two sword cuts in his arm. I saw hundreds of the enemy dead on the field.'

" So much for Golab Rai's story. — He had a cut on his thumb, and asked for a little brandy. I asked how much; half a bottle was the reply. He took this down almost at one gulp. As he had been in the saddle about twenty-four hours, and fighting into the bargain, it will do him no harm. I sent him to my Sikh escort to get his supper, and took his news, a letter from Mr. Power, and the following original production from my Moonshee, over to Sir Colin's mess tent.

" ' Sir,

" ' We have just returned from the field of battle and pitched our tents, but we have not taken any thing yet, but Mr. Power has ordered to bring *rusud* (supplies) very soon.

" ' The action was commenced at eight o'clock. We found the rebels at Sootia, half a mile in the direction of Mhow from Shumshabad; after having

---

* This excellent officer, who was Captain Hodson's second in command, and right-hand man, sunk under his wound, to the sorrow of all who knew his rare value as a soldier.

fired a few balls they ran away: Captain Hodson's cavalry pursued them for more than two miles, and killed numbers of the rebels. A great many were shot by our guns, two were found hidden in a cave, seven in kurbee (high tall cultivation); they were shot, and two caught who are still alive in our Camp. One of them is a boy of twelve years of age. He says he came to watch his fields, the rebels forcibly took him in their Camp. The other is a man of (full) age. Great number of the enemy was killed. — The loss on our side is nothing, but Captains Hodson and Steel have been wounded, and one European killed. — Five or six native soldiers were killed. — The rebels have run away in the direction of Soonijpoor Ghat. The enemy will find no shelter anywhere, the villagers have been highly oppressed by them, and have refused admittance in their village.

." ' Captain Mc Douall's one leg has been shot off. Captain Hodson has been wounded in his right hand in two places, but not severely. We have taken four guns of first rate from the enemy.

" ' This is first time I have seen a battle; first when I saw ball passing by me I was highly frightened and moved little back, but Mr. Power moved forward, then I followed him, and remained the whole time with Mr. Power.

" ' Our camp is to day at Sootia, which was in the morning in the possession of our enemies.

" ' We are very glad in succeeding in routing totally the enemy; the names of the chiefs are Mooltan Khan and Neaz Ahmud, the former is the inhabitant of Mhow, the latter of Bareilly; the men who have been caught alive say half of the rebels were inhabitants of Mhow, Shumshabad, and Rajpoor, and half of Rohilcund, under Neaz Ahmud.

"' I am, Sir,

"' Your most obedient servant,

"' MOHUMUD SAEED.*

"' January 27th, 1858. 3 o'clock.' "

I may here insert another account of this affair, given by an impartial native spectator, and intended for the eye of the Nawab of Rampoor in Rohilcund, which was put into my hands by the Commissioner of Meerut. It will tend to show the value of Sir Colin's plan of not letting his left hand know what his right hand was doing. And it will also demonstrate how absurd was the constant howl about secresy, &c., which was raised by ignorant people who wished the Commander-in-Chief to keep them and all the world informed of all his intentions. It amused Sir Colin very much, when in the following month I placed before him this translation of a native news-letter:—

"Furuckabad news : 29th January, 1858.

" This evening the Hurkaruh (messenger) who was sent to the camp on Monday 25th January,

* This man was educated either in the Government or Mission College at Furuckabad, and is, as may be seen by his letter, which I give *verbatim* and *literatim*, a fair English scholar. Part of his family joined the rebels ; he came over to me at Agra, declaring that he would live no longer at Furuckabad amongst rebels. He is one of the numerous instances of loyalty to the English resulting purely from an English education.

reported thus:—I reached Bareilly on Monday evening. Neaz Ahmud had sent for a convoy of ammunition, so I (the Hurkaruh) went with the Magazine, which was loaded on elephants and camels, from Bareilly to Soorajpoor Ghat, which they reached on Tuesday, and crossed at once to the army of Neaz Ahmud. His camp was pitched six or seven *koss** from Furuckabad. Neaz Ahmud ordered for to-morrow an attack upon Furuckabad.

" On Wednesday (January 27th) before the preparations for an attack were complete, the horsemen on picket duty rode in to say, ' The English are upon us, look out for yourselves.' Before this side could get ready the English came up.

" This side began to fire cannon. The English came on without returning a shot. When they got within range, the first shot† knocked over a gun-carriage; the second shot went right into the mouth of one of the Bareilly guns, so that was also silenced; the third blew up the powder-magazine; another knocked over the treasure chest; lastly, General Neaz Ahmud's horse was shot, the army began to run, and was followed up to the Ghat by the English. I also ran for my life, with the rest, and have just reached Rampoor viâ Bareilly. I can't say what has become of the army, nor how many were killed, but they have been

---

* A koss is about 1¾ mile in this part of India.

† The artillery was commanded by Captains Remmington and Blunt. Their practice, as usual, was rather good.

I

entirely beaten and broken.   Neaz Ahmud Khan
was wounded in two places, and his nephew was
killed.   To the best of my calculation, the Bareilly
army numbered from eight to ten thousand, and
the English two thousand fighting men.   When
roll was called on this side at Ooseyt, twelve hundred men were missing."

The papers* taken in the field by Mr. Power enabled me to lay before Sir Colin a pretty accurate
statement of the resources of the enemy.   They
were full of complaints that the Hindoos along the
left bank of the Ganges were in league with the
English.

"*Saturday*, 30*th*.—In order to protect the river
Ghats, I determined to call out yeomanry levies,
as it was impossible to get soldiers, or good policemen.   I accordingly summoned some of the bravest
Rajpoot clans, who, during the last six months

* Amongst other quaint documents was the following charm,
taken from the dead body of the General's nephew, which was
left on the battle-field.

1	14	11	8
12	7	2	13
6	9	16	3
15	4	5	10

Thirty-four, count it as you like.

had been on their own account, and in self-defence, at war with the rebel Nawab of Furuckabad.

" These men, on the promise of good pay, were only too happy to watch Sheorajpore Ghat, Mhow, Shumshabad, Rajpore, &c. &c. I had four hundred of them posted at once.*

" They have their own arms, and vow they will not allow a rebel to cross the river. They understand that their services are merely required *pro tempore*, and the arrangement suits them. The head man is to have 100 rupees per mensem as Thanadar (chief of police), his Jemadars (or sergeants) are to have 20 rupees, privates 7 rupees. Thus, these unruly spirits and strong hands are enlisted on our side, and we shall have not only their sympathy, as before, but also their aid for the future.

" I forwarded the following information, which I obtained through Mr. Capper †, to Sir Colin.

" 'THE BILGRAM HURKARUH.

" ' Left Lucknow on the 22nd.

" ' Shekh Dost Ally, commandant, still hankering after Menra and Jussomalnow ; the Tehseeldar pressing for revenue ; the people refusing.

" ' A large force still at Lucknow, but disorgan-

* Up to the time I left India, these men had done excellent service, and effectually guarded the river, &c.

† Mr. Capper was a Deputy Commissioner in Oude before the mutiny, and was noticed, for his gallant conduct during the siege of Lucknow (into which place he with difficulty escaped), by General Inglis. His ability and local knowledge were of great value to us all.

ised ; no man will go out to fight a second time ; the only combatants being the mutineers, who are now desperate.

" 'These mutineers have chief authority in Lucknow, and have forbidden 'making beef';* they have well fortified the Begum's Palace in the Kaisarbagh, having built a double timber wall and filled in the interval with mud; many guns are already in position, and they daily cast more ; all the *big guns* have been taken into Kaisarbagh, leaving none out. There are certainly about 30,000 Sepoys on duty at the Kaisarbagh.

" ' On the 23rd, two Sowars from Bareilly brought in a letter from Khan Bahadoor Khan.

" ' The Chukledar publishes that the Punjab army has mutinied, and having already taken Delhi is marching down.

" ' Two Nujeeb regiments and some guns (not known how many), have reached Husungunge. Lukhawut Hossein (the faithful Zemindar of Alrowlee) has seen them; Sufdur Alee Risaldar has returned to Bilgram; some say he is waiting for orders from the Nana.

" ' There are no guns at the Ghats, and the Sepoys are badly off for powder and lead.

" ' The Shahjee about the 23rd attempted to seize the Government at Lucknow ; the Queen Mother resisted ; and they fired big guns and muskets at each other; the Shahjee was defeated, and a large portion of the city was looted, the

---

* The killing of cows.

fight having been in the Chouk. It is not known where the Shahjee is.

" ' Mohamed Hoseen Khan, who was defeated at Goruckpore, is recruiting at Sanda (near Fyzabad), and at the special request of Man Sing, six regiments of mutineers and a battery have been sent down to him from Lucknow.

" ' The following may be relied on : —

" ' The Nana's force (now increased to about 2000 men), is at Seetulgunge, (about five and a half koss from Bangurmow), but his own whereabouts is uncertain. He has engaged many men resembling him in face and figure, and is always in disguise. To ask whether he is in the camp is punishable with death.

" ' The Nana sent a man to Bareilly on the 27th, and a second to Furuckabad.

" ' At Lucknow want of coin is much felt; the nobles are melting down all their plate, and even the religious ornaments are used for pay of troops.

" ' January 28th, 1858.'

" Rode to see Hodson, he is much cut up about McDouall's loss, but treats his own wounds very lightly. Being in his sword arm, we shall lose his invaluable services for a time."

———

Here I take leave of my journal.

It was not my lot to see much more of the stirring scenes passing around. On hearing from Sir Colin that there was a probability of an

advance on Oude, without making any further demonstration upon Rohilcund, in the first moments
of bitter disappointment, I applied (somewhat
impulsively) for the only office which in my
opinion (and, I believe, in the opinion of the
Commander-in-Chief), could have enabled me with
due regard to his service and to my own position,
to accompany His Excellency beyond the limits of
my own (the North-Western) Provinces. In these
provinces my authority was for the time being
paramount, but across the river in the Oude territory I had not any jurisdiction whatever. I therefore asked Lord Canning, if it seemed fit, to constitute me Agent to the Governor-General with the
Commander-in-Chief. I explained that I was receiving overtures from the Oude people, but that of
course I could hold no sort of communication
with them without his Lordship's sanction.

Before I received any reply, the Commander-in-
Chief made a rapid visit to the Governor-General,
at Allahabad, and I, with his permission, brought
my family from Meerut to Cawnpore. Here, on the
24th of February, I took leave of Sir Colin Campbell, Lord Canning having, for doubtless very good
and sufficient reasons, declined to accede to my
proposition to accompany the Commander-in-Chief
as Agent to the Governor-General.

Putting aside the state of my health and my
private affairs, which rendered my return to
England desirable, I bowed to the decision of the
Governor-General with deep regret. It was impossible not to feel more than ordinary pain at

leaving Sir Colin Campbell. Not only had his courage, skill, and justice, won the unfeigned respect of every officer in the service of the East India Company under his command, but his hearty, frank, and cordial nature at once commanded the affection of those who, like me, had the good fortune to be in unreserved communication with him. To make further remark on a personage who I trust may long be spared to us, were superfluous; to say less, impossible.

I had opportunity enough to watch the workings of a mind in which duty was the sole law. It was a fortunate circumstance, due to the personal characters of both, that so perfect a cordiality existed between the Governor-General and the Commander-in-Chief.* Their views may not have been identical as to the line of policy to be pursued, but whatever Lord Canning thought should be done, that Sir Colin delighted to execute.

I have seen in the public prints animadversions

* Sir Colin gave me the following account of the reported " *misunderstanding* " between him and the Governor-General, which once caused serious public uneasiness, and resulted in explanations in Parliament : —

One sultry evening, not long after Sir Colin's arrival in Calcutta, where he was the guest of Lord and Lady Canning, Sir David Baird reminded him that dinner was just coming on the table. Sir Colin had been writing despatches all day, was too tired to make a regular dinner toilette, and, taking Sir David by the arm, strolled across to a neighbouring hotel, where they took a quiet chop and bottle of claret.

The next day it was all over Calcutta that Sir Colin had so serious a misunderstanding with Lord Canning that he had actually left Government House.

on the conduct of civilians who are said to have interfered with the Commander-in-Chief. I can only say, that no civilian in a state of mental sanity would for one moment have ventured to make any suggestion to Sir Colin, other than a mere recital of facts which it was necessary for the Chief to know. But if it is meant that the Supreme Civil Power dictated measures of imperial policy to the head of the army, then I can only say, that Sir Colin was the first man to accept the duties of a soldier, and the very last to question the authority of the State.

It is not for me to discuss what may have been Sir Colin Campbell's views regarding the move upon Rohilcund or upon Lucknow in January last, —that was a matter between His Excellency and the Governor-General in Council. But I may briefly state my own opinions.

I had every personal reason to desire earnestly the advance on Rohilcund. This would have kept me with Sir Colin, and in a position as Civil Dictator, which any man might covet. If this advance had been made at once, soon after Sir Colin's arrival at Futteygurh, the consequences would have been important, so far that our Government would have been then restored without any formidable opposition in Rohilcund.

But the operations against Lucknow would have been delayed, and the rebel or mutineer force in Lucknow much strengthened by the accession of the Rohillas. If, then, Sir Colin could have disposed of the Rohilcund affair, as I think he desired, and as perhaps he might, in all January and February, there would still have been time to go at Lucknow. But there was no certainty that Rohilcund could be so soon disposed of, and for reasons of imperial policy it was absolutely necessary that Lucknow should at latest be attacked in March ; therefore, on the whole, however much opposed to my private interests, I must allow that the policy pursued has been as sound as it has also proved successful.

I had frequent conversations with Sir Colin as to the issue of a proclamation on his advance into Oude. His expression was, that he desired a public proclamation to form his advanced guard on his re-entering Oude. We always believed that any such notification from the Supreme Government would simply announce to the people that the irresistible British army had come to punish all mutineers, rebels, and traitors, but not to carry war to the homes of the people.

In alluding to this proclamation, in conversation with Lord Canning, I understood from his Lordship that the only difference of opinion between himself and the Commander-in-Chief was whether the proclamation should precede, as Sir Colin proposed, or as the Governor-General preferred, follow immediately the actual re-occupation of Lucknow.

Without offering an opinion on the notification which has caused so much discussion in England, I would remark, that in time of war the people of India care very little what is proclaimed ; they look to acts, not to words. If we can beat our enemies in the field the people will accept our policy* without further question. What that policy should be I now proceed to discuss.

I gladly bring the personal part of my narrative to a close ; indeed I should not have considered these passages worthy of the public eye, but for the support which they may give to the opinions which I am about to offer to the consideration of my countrymen.

---

* To speak technically as a revenue officer, the real blot in the proclamation, one entirely overlooked in the parliamentary discussion, was not so much the threatened confiscation of the landed property of rebellious Talookdars, as the cession of full rights in their holdings to certain men named in the notification. The Governor-General had no legal authority to guarantee rights or privileges to these persons without specific reservation of the allodial rights of the subordinate occupiers of the soil.

CHAP. XI.

EARLY in September, whilst we were still nearly confined to within the walls of the Agra Fort, the Lieutenant-Governor desired me to draw up a scheme for restoring the Police of the North-Western Provinces.

I submitted a rough note, which formed the outline of a more complete Report elaborated by Major Williams, Superintendent of Police. The whole plan thus improved was, as I understand, sanctioned by Lord Canning before I left India. I quote here the memorandum submitted to Mr. Colvin on the 5th September, 1857 * : —

" The late disturbances have been caused :

" First. By a general mutiny of the Native Army.

" Secondly. By the violence and rapacity of the Goojur, Mewattie, and other clans, disposed in the best times to predatory habits; also by the cruelty of the lower town-mobs and cantonment rabble.

" Lastly. By the attempts of certain quasi-royal

---

* Slightly enlarged.

pensioners and landholders to revive their lost local ascendency.

" We can hardly expect the Police to come up to the mark of regular soldiers, but if organised, with some important modifications, in the manner of the Punjab Police, a very efficient body might be raised, capable of putting down all local disturbances, and of making the internal Civil Government generally independent of the regular Army.

" In these provinces, the public peace has been preserved, treasuries guarded, and despatches of treasure from one station to another escorted by the Sepoys of the Bengal Native Infantry.

" In order to dispense entirely and for ever with these guards, who have not only failed us in the hour of need, but have themselves placed our empire in jeopardy, I propose that an 'organised Police Force, Horse and Foot,' should be at once raised. Of the material I shall speak presently, merely premising that it should differ from the late Bengal Army *in toto*.

" For each district something like one hundred horse and four hundred foot organised Policemen should be enlisted.

" The horsemen should receive not less than 20 rupees and not more than 25 rupees per mensem, finding their own horses, and generally armed and equipped on the model of the Punjab Police, as organised under Sir Henry Lawrence, Sir John Lawrence, General Chamberlain, and other competent authorities.

" The foot Policemen should receive the rate of pay lately enjoyed by the Bengal Sepoy.

" We should thus have under the Commissioner of each division a force of about five hundred horse and two thousand foot organised Policemen, commanded by a Captain or a Major of the line, who would ordinarily be quartered at the Commissioner's Station, the head-quarters of the Division, and who would superintend the entire divisional organised Police Force.

" A Lieutenant of the line should drill and dress the detachments of these men posted at the Sudder or chief station of each district. His head-quarters should ordinarily be with the Magistrate, to whom he should be attached as an assistant or joint-magistrate. This Lieutenant, with the concurrence of the Magistrate, should have power, on proceedings duly held and recorded, to dismiss any private Policeman, without appeal. *No Court-martial should be allowed.* In like manner, the Commissioner and divisional Commandant should have power to dismiss any native non-commissioned officer. Native commissioned officers (who should, as far as possible, be native gentlemen of family) should only be liable to dismissal by the orders of the local Government.

" The location and disposition of the police force would rest with the Magistrate, subject to the orders of the Commissioner.

" Tour of duty of the same detachment of police, never to exceed three years in any one district.

"Material.

"It is far easier to propose a fitting organisation for a police force, than to decide upon the material of which such a body should consist. The native police of the North Western Provinces have proved unfaithful to their salt, when opposed to mutinous soldiers of their own country, and the higher the organisation of such police, the readier have they been to set up as mutineers, and hurry to join the revolted Sepoys at Delhi.* The organised police in Oude have behaved as badly as the regulars, and if we had been unfortunate enough on this side of the Ganges to have entertained any such force, our dangers and difficulties would have been so far increased.

"We have learned now from bitter experience, that in India, as elsewhere, the people of the country can only be kept in subjection by strangers through the instrumentality of a *foreign* army. We can no more hold these provinces by native troops, without a preponderating power of English or other foreign soldiers, than Austria could hold Italy by Italians, or France hold Africa by African soldiers alone.

"For police purposes we cannot be supplied with European soldiers, so we must look for the next best material at hand.

"Without going into too minute ethnological

---

* The jail guards, who were drilled and dressed in uniform, were the first to turn against their employers.

details, I may just observe that for such a province as Rohilcund, where the Mahomedans have proved treacherous, and for some time to come may prove turbulent, we should use regiments of organised Police embodied on the plan of the Punjab Guides, but with a strong dash of Hindoo or quasi Hindoo tribes, such as Dogras, Sikhs, Muzubees, Goorkhas and Keechees.

" For the Benares Province where there is a dense Hindoo population, there might be a stronger infusion of Afghans, Beloochees, or Punjab Mahomedans. Such men as form the Puthan element in Coke's Punjab Guides, would sympathise as little with the people, and put down an émeute in Benares, as easily as a dragoon from Hounslow or Aldershot, and with much less expense to the State. It may be possible to get mounted riflemen from the Cape, and stout Africans from Sierra Leone, or the Gambia River, as employed in our West India regiments, and I need not point out that the vigour of the former, and docility and strength of the latter, would make them invaluable soldiers in India, though better suited for the regular army than the Police. Lastly, a proportion of Rajpoots from Rohilcund, Aheers from Mynpoorie, Jats from Allygurh, and other tribes who have behaved so admirably during our late troubles, might well be amalgamated with the alien masses already described."

So much for the organised Police, and now to turn to the Rural Constabulary Force:—

" In the higher divisions, *i.e.* nearest the Punjab,

I would absorb the old Khalsa Sikhs as far as they will go, thus conferring a benefit on the Punjab and North-Western Provinces alike. The rest should be of the Hindostanee portion of the material above indicated.

" The military officers in charge of the organised Police should be required to keep one-fifth part of the Rural Constabulary Force under drill, at District head-quarters.

" They should be taught to use the old flint and steel fire-locks, and undergo a modicum of drill, just enough to teach them to move together, load, fire, and march in order."

I was to have discussed this scheme with the Lieutenant-Governor on the 7th of September last, but he was too ill to see me, and on the 9th he died.

At a subsequent period I notified to Government my cordial approbation of a system of yeomanry levies, which I think was first proposed by that accomplished officer, Mr. Edward Anderdon Reade, senior member of the Revenue Board at Agra. On this subject some information will be found in Chapter X., where I have described the practical use I made of yeomanry levies when Civil Commissioner with Sir Colin Campbell.

The scheme thus hastily sketched would give for the North-Western Provinces, exclusive of the Delhi Division (which has been made over to the Punjab), the following force:—

27 Districts, each 100 Horse   -   2,700 Police Sowars.
   Do.   Do.   400 Foot   - 10,800 Police Foot.

I have put down twenty-seven districts, because the district of Goruckpore, with a population of three millions, *must* be divided into two Zillahs.

This force will keep the public peace in our North-Western Provinces easily when once order has been restored, and will furnish guards for all public offices, treasuries, jails, convoys, &c.

The regular army, relieved of these duties, may safely be reduced in proportion.

Thus far I have dealt with a question familiar to my mind. In proceeding to offer a few suggestions on matters of a more purely military nature, I ask indulgence.

The military force which should, in my opinion, suffice to hold the North-Western Provinces in their present state, with the aid of an organised Police Corps, I set down thus:—

Civil Division.		Cavalry.		Infantry.
Meerut	-	2000	-	4000
Rohilcund	-	2000	-	4000
Agra	-	1500	-	4000
Allahabad	-	1500	-	4000
Benares	-	1500	-	4000
Grand total		8500		20,000

With an organised Police Force two-thirds of the military would be available for service in any direction. But for service beyond the Peninsula of India it would be prudent to employ Asiatics, in other words, to take away as few Europeans as possible.

K

The proportion of military and organised Police Force to the population should be gradually reduced in the North-Western Provinces from the standard here given to about one thousand foot, and two hundred and fifty horse, for each million. Thus, the proposed regular army of horse and foot for the North-Western Provinces might be gradually lowered to eighteen thousand foot, and four thousand five hundred horse, leaving the organised Police at the full numbers originally proposed.

The proportion of Europeans to native soldiers need not exceed one-fourth of the regular military force. Thus, for the provinces under notice, we should require eventually only four thousand five hundred British infantry and about eleven hundred cavalry.

This proportion might be reduced by the employment of Africans, such men as are now enlisted for service in our West India regiments, who would stand the climate well, and are celebrated for docility, physical strength, and temperate habits. And of the European portion of the force one-fourth might be Germans, Italians, or Swiss mercenaries, so far as Indian considerations are concerned.

I leave it for more experienced hands to fix the number of artillerymen required. The force must be a powerful one. When right is on our side, as I trust for the future it will be in India, there is no such diplomatist as your twenty-four pounder. Whatever the artillery force may be, one precaution seems indispensable. All and every sort of great gun should be kept in the hands of Europeans, and Europeans alone. The natives of India should have nothing to do with the preparation, manipulation, or custody of our ordnance stores. Strict precautions on this head, such as were originally* introduced by the Court of Directors (so far as the natives are concerned), would at once infinitely increase our power and lessen our danger in India. Guns are to the natives what ships are to Great Britain. The possessor of the strongest artillery is the master of India; and although we can generally take their guns, and the natives seldom indeed have managed to deprive us of our artillery in open fight, yet, to restore our prestige and to maintain it, we must be clearly masters in this respect.

For laboratory duties Africans would be available, and should at once be employed.

On the number of guns and artillerymen kept up by native independent Powers, we should keep a jealous eye; and in independent States we should positively restrict, if possible, the accumulation of cannon, sulphur, shot, or shell.

To enable the Magistrate to do his duty, the inhabitants of our own territories should be disarmed, and an Act similar to the Punjab Arms Act sternly enforced.

The future constitution of our native regiments in Bengal and the Punjab is an anxious and difficult question.

---

* Bengal Artillery: Calcutta Review, No. 18, June, 1848.

Lately at Delhi all eyes were on "the Guides," who, mounted on camels and dromedaries, came hurrying down to mix in the struggle. The Punjab regiments looked up to the Guides as their model: had they faltered the consequences would have been serious indeed. But, when the Guides, under their admirable officers, plunged boldly into the thickest of the fight, shedding their blood like water for the nation who had so lately deprived them of their national liberty, every Englishman from Peshawur to Calcutta breathed more freely. We saw at once that the Sikhs were on our side ; what the Guides had done, other Punjabee regiments would attempt. The prophecy which Mr. Colvin had made to me in May was to be fulfilled, "John Lawrence and the Sikhs will re-conquer Hindostan."

Now the secret of the success of our Guide Corps, and of some other Punjab regiments made on the same model, and inspired, as I believe, by the genius of Sir Henry Lawrence, is simply this:—

As a rule, each company, or troop, consists of a separate nationality, or of men of one country and native officers of another. Take for example the following analysis of the Punjab Guide Infantry, at a late period:

No. 1. Company comprised all sorts of up-countrymen, i. e. high up in or above the Punjab, under down-country (Poorubeea) native officers. This was familiarly called the Roolla Moolla (olla podrida) company.

No. 2. Puthans from Peshawur, fierce, relentless, and savage-looking.

No. 3. Punjabee Mahomedans from Lahore or Sealkote, from the banks of the Beas, the Ravee, and the Chenab. Tall, sleek, good-natured, quiet men, easily managed in the lines, and ready to cut off the head of a brother Mahomedan in Hindostan when duty required.

No. 4. Khas (pure) Afreedees, speaking Pushtoo.

No. 5. Goorkhas from Nepal, brave little fellows, with high cheek bones, eagle eyes, fond of cricket, shooting, fishing, and fighting.

No. 6. Sikhs, tall, wiry, long-enduring, from the Manjha or mid-country, between the Beas and Ravee.

The Cavalry Guide Corps was composed on the same principle.

In regiments thus constituted there is a perpetual rivalry of company against company, or troop against troop. National as well as regimental jealousies and antipathies prevent combination. Thus we come back to the old lesson, "*Divide and Conquer.*" Had our Bengal army been constituted on this plan no weapon formed against us could have prospered.

In reconstituting our native army, and to some extent in forming an organised Police Force, we must take the Punjab Guide Corps as our model, if we would never drift into mutiny again.

It will not do to adopt the easier and more obvious plan of throwing separate nationalities into distinct bodies. We do not want Indian regiments cemented together by the bond of a common country or faith, but we want regiments composed of various elements, incapable of cohesion or absorption, yet under the strong hand of the European fit for powerful and united action. It is this mixture of unity, as a whole, with diversity in the component parts, which gives the perfect organisation. Such a body is safe to the State, and terrible to the enemies of the State alone.

Separate regiments may revolt and do mischief any day, but a separate troop or company can hardly rise in mutiny, because the other troops or companies would at once combine to cut off the offender.

But as it will be found practically impossible to carry this mode of organisation out in every case, we must, as the only safe alternative, grasp still at the principle here set forth. If we cannot have enough mixed regiments, then to make up the deficiency, the Punjab must garrison Hindostan, Hindostan the Punjab.

The latest researches of our best antiquarians show that the old Romans employed the levies from one province to hold the garrison of another. We must to some extent do the same. A Sikh will not mutiny at Benares, to run the gauntlet thence to Lahore amidst a nation of enemies. Neither will the men of Hindostan try a second time the experiment of running from Lahore to Benares.

A few words in conclusion on the character of the British officer who is to lead these regiments, and who, instead of being thwarted by a system of centralisation, should have full power over his men. Sir Henry Lawrence's system being the best for our purpose in forming a regiment, we may take Sir Henry also as our model of a regimental commander. The Friends of M. Guizot called him " *un rosier en fer*;" this is just the description of what Sir Henry was, of what his bosom friends, Lake, Reynell Tayler, and Robert Napier still are. Men of this stamp have a marvellous power over rough natures; but whether we have the " *rosier*" or not, the "*fer*" is absolutely indispensable in a leader of Sikhs or Afreedees. The almost superhuman power of Nicholson over the Sikhs was to be found in a perfectly just, yet relentlessly firm temper, and a bold and noble presence. " The tramp of his war-horse might be heard two miles off." Such was the description given of Nicholson by a rough Sikh who wept over his grave. A mere easy, good-natured man, who can only be *nurum* (soft), and never *gurrum* (hot), will not do for the Sikhs. The mixture of quiet benevolence and justice, with an ardent spirit, chains them to a leader for ever.

CHAP. XII.

RELIGION AND EDUCATION.

I PROCEED now shortly to consider the duties of the British Government with regard to religion and education in India.

The mysteries of the native mind have been so far disclosed during the revolt, that it seems less difficult by the light thus given to discuss the great and kindred questions of religion and education. If one fact was, during the late troubles, more clearly demonstrated than another, it was this, that the body of the natives hated our system of village schools, whilst they clung to our colleges. The reasons for this preference and aversion appear to be these: The village schools were generally supported by a subscription of one per cent. on the Government revenue. The influence of local officers was enough to induce the landholders to grant this cess, but at heart the ignorant Zemindars looked upon the whole scheme with suspicion and aversion, as calculated to interfere with their religion and their pocket at the same time.

On the other hand, the payments to the colleges were purely voluntary; and the education given in the English language, and in the missionary colleges in the Christian doctrine, had the effect of enlisting the affections of the students. The boy, who had been instructed in the morality of the Gospel, and had tasted the literature of the West, grew up as a man into the admirer and often the partisan of the English. During the course of the mutiny, numerous English scholars who had offices under our Government came in to us at Agra, from Oude, Rohilcund, and the Doab. All evinced a spirit of determined loyalty to their British employers, and many suffered death merely as English scholars, at the hands of the mutineers. A Bengalee Baboo* at Furuckabad or Cawnpore, was almost in as great peril as a Christian, so long as those cities were in the hands of the rebels. Not that the Baboo had personally any taste for the honours of martyrdom; for to tell the truth, he was the veriest coward under the sun, but simply because the Sepoy instinctively hated the English scholars, as part and parcel of the English community. But the students of Agra, Furuckabad, Benares, Delhi, or Bareilly, who had been instructed either at the Government or Mission Colleges, behaved in a much bolder manner, and often at the risk of their own lives openly declared their adherence to the British cause.

It is further to be remarked, that it is education in and by the English language, and that alone, which has seemed to chain the student to our fortunes. Some of our bitterest enemies were the

* These men are generally employed as English writers in Upper India.

native doctors and surgeons who had studied European science in the vernacular all their lives.

I here introduce a letter written to me on this subject by the Reverend Principal of the Agra Church Missionary College. It will have weight with those who know, as I do, how entirely free Mr. French is from any bias of mind or professional prejudice :—

"From what Dr. Anderson * tells me of the youths of the Delhi College, and from what I have observed personally of the conduct of my boys in Agra, I have no hesitation in stating it as my conviction, that the result of an English—more particularly of a Christian English education—is to bind to us the hearts of the youth of this country by a link stronger than any other which has been yet discovered.

" The boys' good feeling and well wishing towards the English Government seems to have been almost precisely proportionate to the length of time they had been under our training and the extent to which they had imbibed our religious, moral, and scientific teaching. It was not merely that they professed a hollow attachment to our interests when they saw which way things were likely to turn ; but throughout they showed themselves capable of taking an honest and independent part in the support of those principles of order and just government with which their education had led them to sympathise. When among them, I quite

* Professor of Moral Philosophy at the Government Colleges.

lost the sense of being with those whose interests and whose wishes lay in a different direction from my own."

To the testimony of Mr. French I wish to add my own ; not only in support of what he has here advanced — which, from my own observation, I know to be correct,—but also from the wide acquaintance which I had with native civil officers all over Upper India. I found it to be a general rule, that where you had an official well educated at our English colleges, and conversant with the English tongue, there you had a friend upon whom reliance could be placed. So few were the English scholars amongst our enemies, that it was the custom of the mutineers to burn our intercepted despatches rather than attempt to get them deciphered. They would trust nobody who even knew English. I may be reminded that Nana Sahib's Minister was an English scholar ; but the exceptions are sufficiently rare to prove the rule.

Such then was the conduct of the men whose chief tie to us was an English education. The little body of native converts who had openly professed Christianity identified themselves entirely with their co-religionists, and evinced their sincerity by accepting all the difficulties of our position and throwing their lot heartily in with our own. Their cause and the Englishman's cause was one, and many of them sealed the confession of their faith with their blood.

I conclude, therefore, that this is not the time to press vernacular education on the people. But, the Government should fix a standard of secular education, *including English Literature as a sine quâ non*, and bestow a liberal grant in aid to all schools coming up to that standard.

Further than this, there has been the best encouragement to restore* or keep up, as the case may be, the Government Colleges in which English has hitherto been taught, and every boy at these seminaries should be put through a course of English, *pari passu* with any other branch of education. The village schools may in the North-Western Provinces be left to themselves until the people see the need, and seek for the appliances of a higher course of study.

To turn to the subject of Religion. The worst enemies to Christianity in India have been Christians. So far then it is the duty of Government to provide suitable pastors for the great religious divisions of their servants, that neither Episcopalian, Presbyterian, nor Roman Catholic should by his brutality or ignorance bring discredit upon the profession of Christianity.

Every Indian village has its temple or mosque, and it was a disgrace, happily now forgotten, that for years the soldiers of our armies met to worship

* Wherever Mission premises, libraries, or Churches have been destroyed by the people, at the instigation of the mutineers, it is incumbent on the Government to levy the amount from the district. Sir John Lawrence and Mr. Montgomery did thus at Lodiana, where the people helped the mutineers in doing mischief. They were fined the full amount of damage done, and the money paid over to the Mission.

God in the barrack or the riding school. The Government, especially in the Punjab, have now liberally helped their servants to build Churches and Chapels, and this reproach no longer exists. Let the Hindoo and Mahomedan see clearly that whilst we boldly profess our own, we desire not to constrain their mode of belief; that though we are not indifferent to all religions, we treat all men alike. If we hold India as conquerors, we rule it as moderators. Our vocation is to keep the public peace, not to govern the public mind. If a Hindoo thinks proper to paint his nose with vermilion, to tie his hair in knots, to squander his money on nautch girls, or pagodas, let him do so. But when he wants to sacrifice his infant children to the river gods, to sing filthy songs on the highway, or to stop up his grandfather's mouth with mud and then launch him still living into the sacred stream*, our laws should interfere. In like manner, if the Mahomedan solace his spirit by beating his breast, and calling on his prophet or martyrs in public procession, we should allow the procession to pass on; but when he rushes about sword in hand frantic with drugs and fanaticism, we should take away his arms and put him to cool in the nearest police station. Even so, if under the garb of religion, a minister of Christianity were to offend decency, public or private, the law would strip his gown from the offender.

* These so-called "Ghat-murders" go on daily close to Calcutta, and should be put down whether the Bengalee like it or not.

This is the proper display of the grandeur of Christianity. Let the Mahometan, with the Koran on his breast, and the sword in his hand, slay or circumcise; let the Hindoo coolly excommunicate mankind. It is the privilege of the Christian ruler neither to repel nor to force the human family,—to maintain at the same moment public decency and private opinion.

To turn to the duties of public servants in India.

The public servant of Government, whether military or civil, should not attempt to preach a crusade, or spend his time in exhibiting religious dogmas, or discussing doctrinal points with the natives his subordinates, for this reason above all others, that this is the surest way to make hypocrites, not converts. Let the soldier or civilian assist the missionary with his purse, his counsel, or his prayers, but let him not usurp an office which is inconsistent with his obligations to the State.

Such is the duty of the servants of the British Government in India. The responsibilities of England are far more wide. Every missionary sent to the banks of the Ganges is not only a herald of truth, but also of good government.

So far as the Christian teacher rightly educates the heathen mind, he not only fulfils the great commands of his Divine Master, but also incidentally aids and supports the British rule.

The interests of Christian missions and good government are identical, not antagonistic. In supporting and enlarging missions to the heathen of India, we not only offer to the Almighty our humble and dutiful tribute, but also to the best of our means contribute to the happiness and well-being of the vast country committed to our care.

CHAP. XIII.

NOTHING astonished the earliest European traveller in India so much as the solicitude of the Gentoos for insect life, and their profound indifference to human suffering. Men died by the road-side uncared for, but for bugs and fleas regular hospitals were provided. Without waiting to inquire how far this is the natural result of that peculiar apathy of the Asiatic mind which, abhorring active interference with other men, is not in itself averse to the emotions of pity and benevolence, I pass on to consider what is the duty of the British Government with regard to the sick and afflicted amongst the native population.

The character of the physician is highly esteemed in the East. Every schoolboy knows that it was to an expert English doctor we owed our first step towards independence in Bengal, and every Englishman is looked upon as a "*hukeem*," and invited to prescribe for all sorts of ailments in all sorts of impossible conjunctures.

The people then being ready to receive our aid, we should not be backward in giving it, and indeed

of late years great efforts have been made to insti-
tute dispensaries and hospitals at every large
station in the North-Western Provinces and the
Punjab.

My own experience leads me to suggest that
natives are not fitted *morally* to control these
institutions, and I strongly urge that as far as
possible the actual local superintendence of the
Government dispensaries be henceforth intrusted
to European hands alone.   If medical education is
too expensive in England or Scotland to enable us
to import regular practitioners for this work, we
should look to Germany for men who at a moderate rate of payment would undertake the duties.
The details of such a scheme could easily be
elaborated; a medical examiner at Dresden or
Vienna might be authorised to pass qualified men
into the service, who would find their way viâ
Trieste to Calcutta as fast as their services might
be required.

These remarks may seem out of place here, but
I have seen the hearts of the people so widely in-
terested by a good European doctor, and so
thoroughly alienated by a bad Mahomedan or
Bengalee practitioner, that I consider it a waste
of money, influence, and human life, to go on
educating natives of India for high and independent medical charge.   The difference between a
hukeem or doctor, and a hākim or ruler, is not so
great in the native mind, that we can afford to
have men like Vuzeer Khan* at Agra, raising the

* Chief native surgeon at the Thomason Hospital College.

green flag of rebellion, and Bose* in the Punjab, offending the people by extortion and cruelty. A wider scrutiny would only confirm my position, that if we wished to strengthen our hold on the native affection, it is expedient and proper to employ European rather than native surgeons, to hold charge of Government hospital institutions.

Working on the basis here proposed, namely, European personal superintendence at the Government dispensaries, it would be easy to combine a leper house, a blind asylum, and a poor house, under the same charge, at every civil station in India.

The lepers should be looked after, not only on their own account, but to prevent them banding themselves into gangs, and under the garb of mendicancy, levying contributions on the public. If the Magistrate prevent, as he is bound to do, this disgusting species of extortion, it is only right that he should be able to point to an asylum where (as at Amritsur and some other places) the leper can be comfortably housed, fed, and cared for.

Lastly, with an European functionary in sole and immediate charge of the charitable institutions at each station, the sick and infirm, who too often

---

* Bose was imprisoned for appropriating the fixed allowance for medicine and diet at the dispensary of Buttala in the Lahore Division. The sum he thus fraudulently took was about two pounds per mensem; his salary being some four hundred pounds per annum. This man had been educated in England, and had the highest testimonials for skill. The late Governor-General dismissed him from the service.

perish miserably by the way-side, might be cared for. This duty can hardly be confided to a native. I may be reminded that the Civil Surgeon does perform all the duties here indicated at our larger stations. This is true, but I desire to advocate the following modification of existing arrangements:—We have now a Civil Surgeon at large stations, with an extra assistant (native) surgeon under him. Instead of a native, I would introduce an European to the immediate personal and local charge of the dispensaries, and other charitable institutions, who should be subordinate to the Civil Surgeon.

At small stations, where we have now native extra assistant surgeons, I would have Europeans of the same grade. This would be a great boon, both to the civil officers and to the people. The present race of extra assistant native surgeons too often bring the very liberality of our Government into disrepute.

CHAP XIV.

THE BENGAL SEPOY, HIS CONDUCT AND PUNISHMENT.

In venturing a few suggestions as to the most fitting punishment of our mutinous Sepoys in Bengal, I may be told at starting, " first, catch your Sepoy ;" but I have sufficient confidence in the measures of the veteran General who leads our armies in the North-Western Provinces of India, to believe that the Bengal Sepoy is, sooner or later, a doomed man, and that it is merely a question of time when that doom shall overtake him. The unworthy and misguided native soldiers who have brought such infinite disgrace upon themselves, and caused so much sorrow and suffering to their employers, will ere long be dragged from their hiding places and put on their trial for mutiny and murder. What then must be their doom? This is a question, important not only as affecting the persons of some thirty or forty thousand men, the remnants of our Bengal army, but also as fixing our own future position throughout Asia. In deciding it we have in the first place to consider what is due to ourselves, as the Lords Paramount of India, and to the millions under our sway. That matter settled, we may allow the dictates of generosity to be heard.

To enter then upon this great question. The facts of the case against the criminal are unfortunately too notorious. The Sepoy of Bengal has been treated with justice and liberality. The British Government has not only shown the utmost consideration for his feelings and prejudices, but has also intrusted the public arsenals, forts, magazines, and treasuries to his keeping. In return, forgetful of the obligations of a hundred years, and without the excuse for a Prætorian career which a feeble or selfish civil Government might have afforded, the native soldier has made a blind rush at supreme power. Regiment after regiment has risen to burn and slay. In some places not a single European, man, woman or child, has escaped the fury of the soldiery. To have a white face, to wear the clothing, or even to speak the language of the Franks, has been death. The forts, providentially, have been generally held by our countrymen in spite of treachery and violence; but numerous depôts of arms and treasure in the hands of the native soldiers have supplied them on every side with the sinews of war. The jails in all directions have been attacked and thousands of prisoners set loose to assist in the work of destruction, and to carry to every village the tidings of the Englishman's disgrace. Some regiments, after falling at the feet of their officers and shedding false tears to lull suspicion, have risen suddenly by night to shoot down alike the beardless boy and the worn-out veteran. Others rushing into the quiet English homes, have put all to the bayonet. Some, as at Gwalior, have spared women and children, or only killed them as if by mistake. Others have protected their officers, and even made some show of remorse. But, with exceptions too limited to deserve much notice here, all from Meerut to Benares have deserted their colours, and proved unfaithful to their salt.

It will then be granted that the Bengal army has been guilty of mutiny, the blackest on the long list of military offences, and is punishable at discretion. A plea, however, is urged in abatement of the extreme severity of the law. The prisoner's motives, character and previous services must be considered. Let us allow due weight to the plea, and inquire what it is worth. And first as to the motive. It is urged that the Sepoy's religious prejudices have been insulted, and that this has driven him into mutiny. Now, allowing that the religious feelings of the men may have been worked upon by designing traitors, who thus sought to excuse a scheme of treachery and violence, it is only reasonable to suppose that any honest soldier who really felt himself in danger of religious defilement, would have made known his fears to his commanding officer. A respectful protest against any order offensive to caste prejudices might have been made, and then, without any real humiliation to the officers of the army, the offence might have been avoided for the future, and explained for the past.

But, such was not the conduct of the Bengal Sepoy. He has made no complaint. Accustomed to secret mutinous meetings, led on by delusive hopes of universal power, by the lust of gain and the love of plunder, he has taken advantage of the too easy confidence of his master. Temptation was before him; he yielded, and scrupled not to compass the destruction of the nation, which, for more than three generations had led his forefathers and him-self to victory. We must therefore give no credit to those who seek to excuse the conduct of the Sepoy, as prompted by mere religious enthusiasm.

The truth is, that ever since the reverses at Cabool* first taught the natives of India that an English army might be annihilated, it has only been a question of time with the Sepoys when they should make Bengal, as was Cabool, the grave of the white man.

But again, the Bengal Sepoy pleads long and faithful service. The records of a century prove the truth of the first part of this plea, but it may be questioned whether length of service can constitute any apology for want of faith. It is hardly an excuse for the treacherous servant, who first stabs and then robs his master, that he has been reared from a boy in that master's house. Still, it is argued, the service rendered has been great. Now without pretending to discuss the history of the Bengal Sepoy, I think we may fairly allow that, all things considered, he has done good service. As a mercenary soldier, hired to bring or keep in subjection his own country-men, it is our own fault if we have trusted the Sepoy too much. If we have expected of our

* I have witnessed a marked change in the conduct of the Bengal Sepoys from the period of our Cabool disasters.

armed servants, strangers to our blood and our religion, a degree of fidelity which no Indian potentate expects from his own sons, the fault is our own. The wonder is, not that the Indian soldier has been sometimes the coward, and often the bully or malingerer, but that he has so freely shed his blood in the cause of his employers, and honestly performed his duty so long amidst such great temptations. The earliest performances of Clive's 1st Regiment of Bengal Native Infantry, when first the swarthy Asiatic adopted the scarlet uniform of England, under Colonel Forde at Condore and Masulipatam, may be taken as a fair specimen of the subsequent character and conduct of the Bengal army. At Condore, to use the words of Orme, of whom it has been said by the modern Father of History *, that his narrative is one of the most authentic and one of the most finely written in our language, "the Sepoys, seeing themselves attacked, without cover, by Europeans in front, and the horse and multitude of the enemy's Sepoys gaining their rear, or coming down on their flank, scarcely preserved courage to give their fire, hurried, scattered, and without command; and then immediately broke and ran away to shelter themselves in the village of Chambole, and were followed by the nearest of the enemy's horse."†

Again, after describing the storm of Masulipatam, the same historian writes: — " The Sepoys, who behaved with equal gallantry as the Europeans, as

---

* Macaulay's Essays.   " Life of Lord Clive."
† Book x. vol. iii. page 379.

well in the real, as at the false attacks, had about fifty killed and 150 wounded."*

In short, the Bengal Sepoy, when working with Europeans, shoulder to shoulder, has generally done well; but if unsupported has been apt to take to his heels. In some peculiar times of trial he has set a good example to European soldiers, and even to British officers. For instance, Major Coote, after the battle of Plassy, marched at the head of his Sepoys on Patna, whilst his mutinous European soldiers were ingloriously towed up the river in boats.

So again, in the days of Lord Clive, at the time of the mutiny of the British officers, it was virtually to the Sepoys that the Government had to look to keep the mass of their own officers in order.

On considering the whole case, it seems, then, that though England may not condone or pass over the crime of her mutinous Sepoys, some degree of lenity may with justice be exhibited. It is, however, of the last importance that any mildness which the British Government may practise, should not be mistaken for timidity. We may not forget the genius of the people with whom we have to deal. Moderation and power so rarely go together in their minds, that it is dangerous to yield even to those emotions of pity and generosity for a prostrate foe, which are so natural to every English breast.

The extreme rigour of the law should be enforced against every man in regiments which dyed their hands in the blood of our countrymen. In such

† Book xi. vol. iii. page 489.

cases there is no room for remorse,—justice demands the victim and mercy would be out of place.

Regiments that have gone into mutiny unattended by bloodshed, should receive a milder but still a severe punishment. If after mutiny the men of such corps in a body joined our enemies in the field, their punishment should be perpetual imprisonment, with hard labour, in transportation beyond the seas.

Lastly, men, who having deserted their colours, betook themselves quietly to their homes, should also be sent out of India, but (if I may venture a crude suggestion) rather as emigrants than convicts.* Offenders of this class might be sent to any place where the resident colonists desire to

---

* I make the following extracts from my journal to show the conduct of some of our troops at the time of the mutiny.

Major Raikes described the mutiny of his troops of cavalry thus :—

Hindoo Singh Kechi Russaldar (native officer of the Kechi caste, from the neighbourhood of Gwalior) told the Major not to go to the lines, for the men had sworn not to move. He and some other native officers escorted Major Raikes to within eight miles of Agra, crying and saying they were ruined; but into Agra they would not go ; for, said they, all the men say we shall become Christians if we go to Agra. The Kechis were all on Major Raikes's side, but were threatened with death, to their women and children, by the Mahomedans of the regiment.

In Major Burlton's corps (also Gwalior Contingent Cavalry,) the troopers on going into mutiny actually paid the bazaar debts of an officer's servant, to the regimental sutler, to enable the man to go off with his master.

Again, Major Mackhenzie, of the 8th Irregular Cavalry, told me that his Russaldar, Mahomed Nizam (now Sirdar Buha-

have their services, and they might be declared entitled to liberty in their new homes after a certain period, say seven years of good conduct; but, neither in this case nor in any other, should a convicted mutineer be allowed to return to India. Each and all should be branded, and the punishment for escape or attempt at escape, death.

If this is severity, the reason is sufficiently obvious. If any native of India, who having once eaten of our salt, has lifted his hand against us, be permitted under the shade of his village groves to boast of his exploits against the ruling power, there is so far an end to our prestige. Either mutiny must be connected in the mind of our subjects with death, whether social or physical, or we shall have more mutinies. Severity is the truest mercy in this case, and the only safety.*

door), when a mile or two out of Bareilly in the retreat to Nynee Tal, was told by the Major to go back and look after his three motherless boys, who were left in the lines of the mutineers. The old man answered, " Give me your hand;" then looking up to heaven with tears in his eyes, he exclaimed, "I will go on with you and do my duty." I had heard of these children when I was at Futtygurh and sent to see them; they had suffered much from poverty and neglect. I would remark, once for all, that thousands of the Sepoys were driven into mutiny unwillingly by the bad characters of each corps, who killed the favourite officers in order to compromise their associates, and thus prevent the only influence which could stay the disaffection.

* The 20,000 Sepoys *detenus* in the Punjab should, as each province thoroughly settles down, be drafted gradually to their own homes.

CHAP. XV.

THE CHARACTER OF THE LATE REVOLT.

THE reader who has followed me thus far, is aware that I attribute the origin of our existing disturbances in India to a mutiny in the Bengal army, and to that cause alone; I mean that the exciting and immediate cause of the revolution is to be found in the mutiny. That we have in many parts of the country drifted from mutiny into rebellion, is too true; but I repeat my assertion, that we have to deal now with a revolt caused by a mutiny, not with a mutiny growing out of a national discontent. I shall here, with reference to the facts narrated in the earlier chapters of this work, attempt to prove the above assertion.

In the first place, I should not have offered my services to the Lieutenant-Governor to proceed to Mynpoorie as a recruiting officer, to live as I had intended in the villages of that district, unless I had positive knowledge of the good feelings of the people in May 1857.

To proceed a little later to a different part of the country, and to other native tribes, Messrs. Phillipps and Bramly, civil officers of considerable position and experience, arrived at Agra on the 10th of June, having traversed the country from

Furuckabad, and Etah in the Doab, and from Budaon in Rohilcund, with a very small escort of three or four horsemen. They had been travelling for nearly a month amongst the villages, and on their arrival at Agra declared, as I find entered in my journal, that " the villagers are all on our side, except some of the Mahomedans."

During this same entire month of June, Mr. Arthur Cocks, the Judge of Mynpoorie ; Mr. Watson, the Magistrate of Allygurh ; Doctor Clark, young Mr. Outram of the Civil Service, Mr. Herbert Harington, and a few others, heroically maintained their position, at or near Allygurh, after the mutiny and destruction of the station. It was because the people of the country were with and not against us, that this handful of volunteer horsemen were enabled to hold the post amidst swarms of mutineers passing up the grand trunk road to Delhi.* The same thing went on in August and September; generally wherever the Sepoys or low Mahomedan rabble were not, the English were safe. Some villagers, robbers by prescription, tradition, birth, and education, turned against us ; but after the fall of Delhi, and a short taste of anarchy, the bulk of the people

---

* Their head-quarters were at Allygurh. When the villagers gave them notice of a large body of Sepoys coming up towards Delhi, they used at night to shift their quarters three or four miles, the mutineers at the same time often making a detour of twenty miles to avoid the volunteers. When large bodies of the Mahomedan citizens raised the green flag and swore to kill the infidels or perish in the attempt, a charge from the volunteers soon quelled their enthusiasm.

were glad to see a white face, even in the person of a revenue collector.

In order to apprehend rightly what was the feeling, as well as the conduct of the mass of the people when the mutiny broke forth, a short analysis of the component parts of the human mass in the North-Western Provinces may be useful.

The male population was divided into the following classes : —

Hindoos.

Agricultural	- - - - -	9,549,192
Non-Agricultural	- - - -	4,254,453

Mahomedans.

Agricultural	- - - - -	996,950
Non-Agricultural	- - - -	7 9,941
	Total - -	16,180,536

Now, of these sixteen millions, not one-twentieth part resided in districts which had any European soldiers stationed within their limits. The mass of the people knew and acknowledged the supreme power of their English masters, but they attributed that power entirely to the bayonets of the Bengal Native Infantry, which held the forts, arsenals, and treasuries, throughout the country.

Therefore, when the native soldiers rose, as one man, to burn and slay, to pull down the halls of justice, and to break open the jails, the people at large, who knew little and thought less of the distant resources of England, concluded naturally enough that our day had gone by.

The catastrophe was viewed with very different

feelings by the various bodies of our quondam subjects.

The predatory class, the Goojurs, the Mewatties, felt instinctively that their day had come. Their natural enemy, the Magistrate, had perished at the hands of the mutineers, or was flying before them, protected only by the people over whom he lately presided. Forthwith they girded on the sword and buckler, seized the matchlock, and sallied forth to pursue their hereditary vocation of plunder. In pursuit of this instinct they played no partizan's part, but with the utmost impartiality robbed alike the straggling European running for his life, or the Sepoy carrying off his booty. As a matter of course, there was an end of police, telegraph, postal communication, and every other symptom of civilisation, wherever these harpies were found.*

The green flag of Mahomed too, had been unfurled. The mass of the followers of the false prophet rejoicing to believe that, under the auspices of the great Mogul at Delhi, their lost ascendency was to be recovered, their deep hatred to the Christian got vent, and they rushed forth to kill and destroy.

But, making deduction for these classes, the great agricultural communities, the Jat, the Brahmin, the Rajpoot, looked on the English race, under whose auspices they had so long tasted peace and security, with unfeigned compassion. Like the

---

* As for the telegraph, it became a favourite engine in the hands of the village marauders, who used the iron sockets (mounted on carts) as guns, and cut up the wire into slugs.

robber tribes, they considered our case hopeless, but unlike them they *at first* lamented lost order.

Such was their first impulse; they showed it in a hundred instances, by helping our straggling countrymen, and protecting them from Sepoys or rabble, often at the risk of their own lives.

But as the course of events hurried on, as Magistrate, Cutcherry, revenue process, subsided alike, these men, who, as forming the bulk of the agricultural class, had been saddled with a very full share of the public imposts, began to think it no bad change if only they could avoid revenue payments for the future.

In common with the rest of mankind they were not fond of paying taxes, nor were they long disconsolate when the tax-collector disappeared from the scene.

If there was no Government, there was no quarter-day.

It requires no special knowledge of India to comprehend the rapid spread of passive disaffection (not active hostility), under such circumstances as these.

When disaffection means more money, more power, and no taxes, its growth is a mere necessity of human nature. There would be a good crop of disaffection in Kent or Somersetshire, under parallel conditions.

But even this natural feeling yielded to a few weeks' experience of anarchy. The Zemindar soon found that it was better to pay land-tax and receive protection, than day and night to fight for his possessions with every scoundrel in the country side. And thus, the bulk of the tax-paying agricultural proprietors in the Doab, after the fall of Delhi, welcomed their English masters back with unfeigned satisfaction.

Still more did the moneyed classes, such of them at least as survived the period of anarchy, rejoice to see the English rule restored. On the retirement of the Magistrate, a furious struggle had commenced at once between the purchasers of land in possession, and the former owners. Native bankers and merchants who had long been investing their savings in land (purchased generally under decrees of court), were either murdered or scared away. The life of a capitalist in possession of land, whether as purchaser or mortgagee, was soon not worth a week's purchase. Old feuds broke out afresh, homicides, affrays, murders by day, by night, gang robberies and arson.* Things grew worse and worse, until, as I have said before, every man but the professional robber or dacoit longed for the return of the Magistrate, notwithstanding the fact that he was also the collector of the Government revenue. The robbers joined the straggling Sepoy bands, and to this day are in arms against us,

* How fare my old friends the Bhyleas? (a class of professional thieves), I asked of the Tehsildar of Shekoabad, who had come to see me at Agra in August. "Sir," he answered, "they are the most respectable class of the community left, but they are all starving." I asked why? The answer was, "When robbers are supreme, mere thieves have no chance."

M

whilst the rest of the people hastened to pay up all arrears of revenue into our treasuries.

Amidst these various modifications of feeling, there was one class amongst our own immediate subjects, which with a few marked exceptions adhered without a shadow of hesitation or double-dealing to our fortunes. I allude to the Talook-dars, or superior holders of considerable landed estates, who received a share of the Government due, and retained some little power and influence as the fading remnants of the native landed aristo-cracy.*

The conduct of these men† suggests reflections

---

* I speak not of Oude, but of the ceded and conquered Provinces.

† It was perhaps to be expected that the Talookdars, who during the siege of Delhi had stood firm to the British Government, should, on the re-occupation of the country by us, open their mouths rather wide, whether to notify their own merits or to receive whatever the Government might think fit to drop therein. I must quote one honourable exception to this general rule in the person of my old and esteemed friend Luchmun Singh, Talookdar of Kurowlie, in the Mynpoorie district. This man had a small fort on the Grand Trunk road, near Myn-poorie. When the lamented Fletcher Hayes was murdered by his own men, Luchmun Singh secured the body, and at the risk of his own life sent it in to Mynpoorie. During the months of July and August, when continually surrounded by muti-neers, he contrived to send me frequent letters concealed by his servants, sometimes in an old shoe, sometimes in a walking-stick.

After a long ride in February last, I arrived somewhat way-worn at his house. One of his servants officiously began the process of "shampooing" my legs; the old gentleman pushed him aside, saying, that was his privilege. Loaded with atten-

with regard to our future policy, which I shall proceed to discuss. I have, I hope, said enough here to satisfy the candid reader that we have had no rebellion, properly so called, in the North-Western Provinces of India, and that the disorganisation caused by the violence of the Sepoys and the consequent temporary withdrawal of the Magistrate, has been merely a passing evil and not a permanent lapse in our career of progress and domination.

tions, when I was starting again on my journey, I said, "What are we to do for you to show our sense of your loyal conduct?" His reply was, "I can't eat more than one dinner daily. I have seen the English back; I want nothing more."

CHAP. XVI.

OUR FUTURE RELATION TO THE PRINCES AND PEOPLE OF INDIA.

In a former chapter, I have described how the Political Agent was compelled to fly from Gwalior. Few know how much we, at Agra, are indebted to Major Macpherson for our immunity from attack by the full force of the Gwalior Contingent, with their powerful siege artillery. The real state of the case was this, the Political Agent had full influence over Scindia's Dewan, or prime minister, the celebrated Dinkur Rao.* The minister, in his turn, influenced his master, and thus Major Macpherson, from the interior of the Fort at Agra, ruled the course of events at the Court of Gwalior. Scindia, by threats, promises, cajolery, and ready money, kept the formidable Contingent Army quiet until October. When nothing could restrain them longer, he contrived to direct their progress away from his own country towards a part of the British possessions where he believed there was a sufficient force to oppose them. He continually applied to us for European soldiers to help him, and, in short, at the

---

* Dinkur Rao is a Bramin élève of the late Sir W. Sleeman. He is the most enlightened native that I have had the good fortune to meet.

undoubted risk of his own power and life embraced the English cause. Holkar, also, behaved faithfully and incurred equal danger for our sake. I have already noted the conduct of the Maharajah of Putialee, and might add a long list of native potentates, who, at the most critical period, risked all in their determination to stand by us. Now, but for this unexpected* devotion to our cause of the foreign powers, our difficulties would have increased indefinitely. Let us henceforth, in order to reward and confirm this fidelity, take every opportunity of declaring our distaste to any future territorial expansion, and explain to every independent or protected State in India, that we prefer faithful allies to doubtful subjects. "It will all be red," said Runjeet Singh to an officer who was pointing out the coloured line denoting British territory, "it will all be red soon." We must prove the King of Lahore wrong in this prophecy, though in the case of his own State it has already come true. I may be told that nobody wants to annex, but mere English readers can have little knowledge how zealously some of the ablest directors of the English

---

* Unexpected I mean in many instances. Golab Singh was well known to me, as well as his son Rhunbeer, the present King of Cashmere, as faithful friends to the British power. I was perfectly certain that they would stand by us, but did not feel the same confidence in Scindia. I remember once being cut short in an attempt to moralise at the Jummoo Palace by Golab Singh, thus: "Maharajah," I said, "the Almighty has given you great power, and I trust"——"My Almighty," interrupted the old King, "is the Company!"

press in India have advocated a career of conquest and annexation.

So much for the princes of India. This is not the place to consider the difficult questions of Contingents, Residents, &c. I merely intend to indicate the ruling principle which should hereafter guide the policy of our Indian Foreign Office.

To turn to the Home Office. Next in rank to the foreign princes of India come the Talookdars of our own provinces. Let us for a moment consider what was the position of a Talookdar, whether in the beginning of the present century in the Doab, or in the middle of the same epoch in Oude. A Talookdar, whether holding, as most of them did, large allodial rights of his own in part of his estates, or whether originally mere contractor of the Government revenue, was a very considerable person. Throughout the North-Western Provinces, at the periods of cession and conquest in the commencement of the present century, the Talookdar was treated tenderly. He was found in possession of vast tracts, often equal in area to a good-sized English county, exercising powers over the life and liberty of a teeming population, who, according to his personal character and temper, looked up to him as their tyrant or their protector. The Talookdar had palaces, forts, troops, and, in many cases, artillery, and exacted not only deference and service, but also all sorts of fines, rents, and perquisites* from his subjects. A man thus powerful

---

* The detail of these cesses would fill a volume ; they ex-

abroad, was not less despotic at home. If a lady of the family went astray, she was fortunate, if discovered, to get off with the loss of her nose, and generally paid the forfeit of her life.

Proud barons like these, whose authority over their people was unlimited so long as they paid a sufficient revenue to satisfy the reigning potentate, naturally clung alike to their power and their land with tenacity, and were not scrupulous as to the measures by which they increased either their power or their possessions.

A severe blow was dealt to this portion of the native aristocracy at the period of the great revenue settlement (commenced by Mr. Robert Mertins Bird, and concluded by Mr. Thomason) in the North-Western Provinces.

A methodical scrutiny into title deeds, genealogical trees, ancient imperial records, as well as into the living history of each family, whether of Talookdars, or of subordinate cultivators of the soil, disclosing, as it did, the abuse of power and opportunity, ended often in the destruction of the influence, and the diminution of the profits, of the higher class. This decadence, however, had been so long shadowed forth in the equal spirit of the laws of the East India Company, that, when the fall came, it was gradual and not unexpected. I mean that gradually we had been inculcating the doctrine of accountability of man to man, and the equality of prince and peasant in the eye of the law; and this

tended from a tax on the pregnancy of a wife to a composition on a religious head-shaving.

new doctrine prepared the Talookdars in the North-Western Provinces for the declension of their status and diminution of their estates. This sort of preparation was gradual, and the work of fifty years' administrative progress.

In Oude, however, the case was different. Under the vilest and most corrupt Administration which even Asia had ever witnessed, the power of the Talookdar had become not only despotic, but to the last degree tyrannical. The action of our British financiers on the revenue-paying classes in Oude, exemplified the legal apophthegm to the letter. " *Summum jus, summa injuria.*" Notwithstanding the remonstrances of men like George Christian, who had never been too prone to extend the powers of the native aristocracy, notwithstanding the palpable impolicy of the measure, it was determined at once and entirely to introduce that perfect equality of man and man, which though forming the just pride of Englishmen in England, could not safely be proclaimed suddenly in the latitude of Lucknow. The Talookdar class all over the country was thrown into a state of collapse. Forty years' possession was treated as nothing, if at that remote period the occupation could be proved or supposed to be proved unjust. Old ejected shareholders, trusting to the clemency and justice of the new reign, streamed from across the border back into Oude, and were at once reinstated into their privileges, or rather were endowed with beneficial interests which they had never even claimed. The women were emancipated; wives sued their husbands for liberty of conduct, village slaves dragged their lords before the petty courts, and the lowest mechanic refused the accustomed manorial perquisite or fee.

The principle of equal justice which dictated this policy was right in the abstract, but the change was introduced too rudely, too suddenly, and with too much haste.

The consequence was that when the mutiny broke out in Oude, the Talookdars rose *en masse* to assist the mutineers.

The *huk-dar's* or rightful owners, who had been placed in possession by the British Government, either surrendered at discretion to the Talookdar, and swelled his ranks, or were hunted and killed like vermin by their village lord, all over the country.

How then are we to treat the Talookdars in future? I can only suggest that without compromising the rights of our humbler and weaker subjects in Oude, we should let the Talookdar down easily, and treat him not only with justice but liberality. The extinction of this class of men is not consistent with the safety or durability of our empire, we have erred, with the best possible intentions, in paying too little heed to the position of the landed aristocracy, and our best plan is to acknowledge our error and to retrieve it. We cannot allow these men to be village tyrants, nor to be, as they desire, superior to the law, but we may make some slight concessions of our own revenue in their favour, and need not busy ourselves to hunt out and prohibit some of the least arbitrary of their manorial perquisites. We must be satisfied with a gradual improvement in the relative position of the baron and his serf, and not insist upon the instant and immediate rectification of every inveterate abuse.

Unfortunately, however, the legislator or administrator, who following the right instincts of humanity strives to improve, regenerate, and support the humbler mass of his fellow-men has in India a thankless and too often an impossible task.

The greatest happiness of the greatest number is not easily achieved, when the greatest number can or will do nothing to make themselves heard, felt, or appreciated. It is hard to help a man who resolutely declines to help himself. And here I leave the further solution of this problem to Robert Montgomery, who will do what man can do, to calm and settle the stormy ocean of politics in Oude. The danger probably now will be, not lest the Talookdars be again trampled into the dust, but lest the million be too readily restored to their (the Talookdars) ill-starred dominion.

Descending in the social scale to discuss the interests of the people at large, I can only say in a few words, what I said at some length before the mutiny.

Our intentions towards India have generally been well inspired, but the fatal error of attempting to force the policy of Europe on the people of Asia, an error which has hitherto, with one grand exception, pervaded our Indian history both military and civil, must be corrected for the future, as it has been atoned for in the past.

The divided system of Civil Government which suits the European genius, the distribution of labour and authority between the financier, the exciseman, the police, and the judicial functionary, must cease throughout India, if we really would pacify and govern the people. The Punjab system of government as introduced by Lord Dalhousie, and carried out by Sir Henry Elliot, the Lawrences, Mansel, Montgomery, Edmonstone, and Mc Leod, is so simple, so powerful, so entirely adapted to the genius of the people, that it must, like truth, prevail, and sooner or later extend over the entire Peninsula. The distinctive features of this system have been portrayed by me on another occasion,* and I believe, but for the opposition of the Legislative Council in Calcutta, that (as suggested by me and pressed on the attention, both of the local and supreme governments,) this simple system would ere now have been introduced as the basis of our future administration in the North-Western Provinces.

For the future then let us have in the person of

---

* I refer the reader who may wish to go further into this subject to (Appendix B.) a letter addressed by me to Mr. Ricketts. Whilst these pages are passing through the press I observe that this gentleman, who has lately taken his seat in Calcutta as Member of Council, is advocating the views I humbly suggested, and which his wide Indian experience has enabled him to test, in the Legislative Chamber. He will not find his task an easy one.

each District Chief, whether he be called Deputy-Commissioner or Magistrate and Collector, or Judge, a full and combined authority in matters of police, revenue, civil justice, and diplomacy. This is what an Asiatic can understand, but his mind can never accept the constitutional idea of a Governor.

Not to waste words further, unless we exert a despotic power in Upper India, we must leave the country and the people to the most frightful state of anarchy which the world ever saw. We cannot even try any longer to rule Asia on the constitutional principles of Europe.* Nobody dislikes the

---

* I have for years sighed over and protested against the absurdity of a free press amongst the natives of India. The English press has done good, and whenever guided by a spirit of patriotism instead of a systematic hostility to Government, will do more. But the native press is an abomination, above all in the eyes of the natives themselves. When I was Commissioner of Lahore, finding myself impotent to control this great evil, I proposed to Government to establish a cheap paper of useful knowledge, which I offered to edit in my own office. This failing, I was driven to the humiliating expedient of establishing cheap lithographic presses in all the jails under me, in order, if possible, to drive the native lithographs out of the market. My reason for this disgust at the native press is briefly told. Hardly a week passed but some native Sirdar or chief came to me with streaming eyes to implore me to put a stop to printed attacks made on his family affairs, which he considered ruinous to his honour. Every police or revenue official was obliged to subscribe to these ruffian prints by threats of being exposed as inefficient, corrupt, &c. Throughout India this mischief prevailed. In February 1857, a native paper addressed the public thus: " Now is the time for India to rise, with a Governor-General who has had no experience of

attempt so much as the Asiatic himself. However much philosophers may sneer, a " paternal despotism " is not only the happiest, but the only regime for India. This is not the place to say more. With a simple, firm, just system of administration, our Hindoo subjects will not only remain, as they have hitherto been, contented, but they will attach themselves to our rule, as the Sikhs, or, at all events, the Punjabees have done already. For their own happiness, as well as for our safety, the country must be disarmed at once, and for ever. The laws regarding adultery must be changed, and as in the Punjab, the adulterer of either sex be treated as a criminal. We must see the police organised, the civil courts purged, and the procedure simplified. Land should no longer be sold for ordinary debts to any decree-holder or judgment creditor, who has not as mortgagee been already placed in usufructuary possession of the soil.

The landed proprietor should no longer be expected to bear all the burdens of the State. Government should no longer fear town mobs; we have seen enough of their impotency now, and should make the trading classes take a fair share of the public imposts. Hitherto, they have enjoyed all the advantages of our settled government, and contributed nothing towards its expenses.

With a few simple changes of this nature, with an army more carefully selected from our numerous subject or allied tribes, with officers, civil

public affairs in this country, and a Commander-in-Chief who has had no experience of war in any country."

and military, fully trusted, carefully watched, and endowed with real power to punish or to reward, we may yet have a good career before us in India. Let us hope that the wounded feelings of our own countrymen may be softened by time and good management. The surest way to elicit the generous sympathies of an Englishman is to extend his powers. You secure his friendship for the native when you place the fate of the native widely under his care. A generous confidence in an English gentleman will do more to secure his hearty care of the people than any system of reports or appeals, however multiplied and complicated, can accomplish. Public officers who abuse this confidence, should at once be removed from the service.

So much for the general form and tone of our government. To revenue matters a very brief allusion will suffice.

I have already said that we should make the moneyed classes bear a share in the public burden. The Government would do well to sell their land-tax to the proprietors wherever purchasers (at twenty years' tax) can be found.* A system of paper money should be introduced. Instead of dabbling in opium manufacture, the State should tax all opium and all tobacco whilst growing in the

---

* Government Savings Banks should be established in every District, and, as far as possible, the existing system of making advances from the Public Treasuries to the agricultural class extended. At present, the needy Indian peasant pays the village banker fifty per cent. for an advance to buy seed; whilst his thrifty neighbour who has saved a few rupees buries them under his hut.

field.   Give a wide margin to the landowners; remember Sir John Lawrence's maxim in dealing
with them — " The milk that the master leaves in
the cow goes to the calf."   Our own prosperity
depends on the prosperity of the people, and above
all of the agricultural people of India.

A few words as to the Mahomedans.   They have
behaved, in the part of India where I had jurisdiction, very ill; so ill indeed, that if the rest of the
population had sympathised with them, instead of
antagonised *, I should despair of governing India
for the future.

* I cannot give a fairer instance of the difference between
the conduct of the Hindoo and Mahomedan people at the time
of the mutiny than was afforded in our own court at Agra. We
had numerous Mahomedans and Hindoos, with a small sprink-
ling of Christians at the bar. With one exception, all the
Mahomedan pleaders left the court; one of them, Sufdur Ali
by name, was hanged by order of Mr. Harington, for plunder-
ing the property of an English officer. The rest gave no assistance whatever to us. The Hindoos, on the contrary, exerted
themselves to protect and secure the property of their English
judges, preserved our horses and moveable property, and did
whatever else they could to show their loyalty and affection.
The Mahomedans either deserted us or joined the rebels. And
so it was all over the north-western provinces, a Mahomedan
was another word for a rebel. The only Mahomedan who behaved well amongst our pleaders in the Suddir Court was
Ahmed Buxh. His history is curious. Originally a trooper in
the 3rd Cavalry, the very regiment which commenced the
mutiny at Meerut; he was deputed to the court to watch some
cause; his extraordinary ability excited the attention of Mr.
George Edminstone, at that time Registrar of the Court. He
advised the trooper to give up his arms and aspire to the
pleader's ' toga.' Ahmed Buxh studied, took his diploma and
certificates, and became the leader of the Agra bar. During

They have been too much trusted, and must be watched carefully hereafter. A certain portion of public appointments should be continued in their hands, proportionate to their numbers, in each district, but they should not be allowed to enjoy too large a share of the Government patronage.

At the same time that we narrowly watch their conduct, we must beware of even tacitly encouraging religious strife between them and the Hindoos. Every ebullition of religious rancour amongst the natives recoils upon ourselves. If we cannot soften we must not exasperate the jealousies of caste and religion.

To conclude, it is impossible too often to reiterate the demand for firmness and gentleness in the personal character of our Indian administrators.

If ever the iron hand in the velvet glove was wanted, it is now.

The East India Company, after placing subject nations at the foot of the Throne, after educating illustrious statesmen, and training victorious generals, is henceforth to live in history alone.

England's Sovereign* is for the first time to wield directly the sceptre of India.

the mutiny he showed such zeal for our cause, that he was accused of being a Christian, and on retiring to his own estates he still gave such aid to the magistrate as to entitle him to the marked notice and thanks of Government.

* This change, so far as it may be known to the people of India, will be hailed with respect. I say, so far as it is known, because the common people never had any very intelligent comprehension of what the Company meant. I recollect asking an intelligent yeoman, a man who paid his annual hundred

The highest aspiration of every Englishman may well be that the future administrators of our Indian empire, whilst inaugurating a bolder* and more successful policy, may, at the same time, emulate the considerate, earnest, and just traditions of the expiring dynasty.

rupees or more of revenue to the State, who the Company was, he said, "I don't know much about the matter, but '*muraroo hogee*' she is a female of some sort!"

* By boldness I mean not only that audacity without which it is impossible to succeed in Indian warfare, but also a bolder assertion of our own religion as Christians, of our own privileges as Europeans, and of our general national superiority. An Asiatic by instinct despises the man who depreciates his own position. We should legislate and govern in India as the superior race. Whenever that superiority ceases, our right to remain in India terminates also.

APPENDICES.

General Statement No. I. Statistical Return of Land, Revenue, Area

Division.	District.	Number of mouzahs or townships.	Area in square British statute miles of 640 acres each.	Area in acres.	Malgoozaree or assessed land.		Minhaee or unassessed land.		Demand on account of land revenue for 1851-52 in rupees.
					Cultivated acres.	Culturable acres.	Lakhiraj acres.	Barren acres.	
1	2	3	4	5	6	7	8	9	10
Dehlie	Paneeput	538	1,269.9	812,745	407,051	261,747	19,398	124,549	8,27,1
	Hissar	653	3,294.2	2,108,279	988,923	864,099	85,528	169,729	4,65,7
	Dehlie	568	789.7	505,320	263,208	76,585	91,402	74,125	4,56,4
	Rohtuck	300	1,340.4	857,885	641,792	147,183	22,730	46,180	6,31,1
	Goorgaon	1,274	1,939.1	1,241,017	895,940	168,428	16,352	160,297	10,47,2
	Total	3,333	8,633.3	5,525,246	3,196,914	1,518,042	235,410	574,880	34,27,7
Meerut	Suharunpoor	1,904	2,162.3	1,383,898	774,253	211,449	54,597	343,599	10,64,5
	Moozuffurnugur	1,138	1,646.3	1,053,641	670,468	153,173	76,287	153,713	11,07,5
	Meerut	1,638	2,200.1	1,408,063	907,758	236,021	82,028	182,256	16,93,0
	Boolundshuhur	1,576	1,823.6	1,167,094	715,587	143,260	88,036	220,211	10,56,8
	Allygurh	1,997	2,153.4	1,378,204	961,076	77,725	41,070	298,333	19,85,1
	Total	8,253	9,985.7	6,390,900	4,029,142	821,628	342,018	1,198,112	69,07,0
Rohilcund	Bijnore	3,030	1,900.0	1,216,005	590,622	175,553	42,626	407,204	11,97,6
	Moradabad	3,484	2,698.8	1,727,216	839,919	308,851	256,086	322,360	13,40,3
	Budaon	2,232	2,401.9	1,537,191	928,299	286,055	69,734	253,103	10,97,3
	Bareilly	3,563	3,119.1	1,996,224	1,056,961	394,810	83,630	460,823	17,69,6
	Shahjuhanpoor	2,785	2,308.4	1,477,359	716,201	453,032	33,067	275,059	10,60,3
	Total	15,094	12,428.2	7,953,995	4,132,002	1,618,301	485,143	1,718,549	64,65,2
Agra	Muttra	1,019	1,613.4	1,032,542	733,362	87,224	97,649	114,307	16,57,2
	Agra	1,143	1,864.9	1,193,537	747,536	118,104	84,460	243,437	16,22,9
	Furruckabad	2,017	2,122.9	1,358,685	749,023	178,345	69,985	361,332	13,33,0
	Mynpoory	1,344	2,020.2	1,292,946	687,098	114,526	8,510	482,812	12,67,0
	Etawah	1,495	1,677.0	1,073,276	557,804	59,927	29,143	426,402	12,72,0
	Total	7,018	9,298.4	5,950,986	3,474,823	558,126	289,747	1,628,290	71,52,4
Allahabad	Cawnpoor	2,257	2,348.0	1,502,699	800,438	149,232	61,992	491,037	21,44,0
	Futtuhpoor	1,617	1,583.1	1,013,171	509,793	131,895	9,417	362,066	14,26,9
	Humeerpoor	997	2,241.6	1,434,651	770,254	316,504	14,531	333,362	12,77,8
	Banda	1,257	3,009.6	1,926,112	846,831	561,281	82,934	435,066	15,91,3
	Allahabad	4,003	2,788.7	1,784,780	971,558	247,255	28,240	537,727	21,41,2
	Total	10,131	11,971.0	7,661,413	3,898,874	1,406,167	197,114	2,159,258	85,80,7
Benares	Gorukpoor	15,714	7,340.2	4,697,706	2,232,901	1,268,024	160,732	1,036,049	21,33,9
	Azimgurh	6,270	2,516.4	1,610,498	798,707	213,729	41,027	557,035	14,89,6
	Jounpoor	3,431	1,552.2	993,383	573,616	58,121	23,497	338,149	12,54,0
	Mirzapoor	5,280	5,152.3	3,297,472	768,296	293,394	1,421,412	814,370	8,39,7
	Benares	2,296	995.5	637,107	420,069	35,791	29,571	151,676	9,03,5
	Ghazeepoor	5,088	2,181.0	1,395,808	924,884	151,168	41,532	278,224	15,00,4
	Total	38,079	19,737.6	12,631,974	5,718,473	2,020,227	1,717,771	3,175,503	81,21,1
	Grand total	81,908	72,054.2	46,114,514	24,450,228	7,942,491	3,267,203	10,454,592	4,06,54,

Population, in Thirty-one Districts of the North-Western Provinces, prepared in 1852-53.

Rate per acre on total area.	Rate per acre on total Malgoozaree.	Rate per acre on total cultivation.	Population — Hindoo. Agricultural. Male.	Female.	Non-agricultural. Male.	Female.	Mahomedans and others not Hindoo. Agricultural. Male.	Female.	Non-agricultural. Male.	Female.	Total.	Number of persons to each square British statute mile of 640 acres each.	Number of acres to each person.
11	12	13	14	15	16	17	18	19	20	21	22	23	24
3 1	3 9	2 0 6	94,360	73,397	49,252	38,802	20,411	16,869	51,643	44,351	389,085	306	2.09
6 0	4 0	0 7 6	113,974	93,170	23,555	17,207	33,638	28,189	12,044	9,075	330,852	100	6.37
5 1	5 6	1 11 9	93,963	77,731	78,912	65,459	10,036	8,881	52,292	48,470	435,744	552	1.16
9 0	12 10	0 15 9	117,168	102,275	61,770	50,610	11,890	12,059	11,451	9,790	377,013	281	2.27
6 0	15 9	1 2 8	174,457	147,726	73,138	65,453	85,314	73,057	22,107	21,234	662,486	342	1.87
11 0	11 8	1 1 2	593,922	494,299	286,627	237,531	161,289	139,055	149,537	132,920	2,195,180	254	2.52
4 1	1 3	1 6 0	155,176	109,146	165,789	125,829	53,281	44,853	79,840	67,431	801,325	370	1.78
10 1	5 6	11 0 10	135,478	105,768	133,273	115,652	44,336	39,607	51,672	47,075	672,861	409	1.56
3 1	7 8	1 13 10	237,105	190,680	245,814	211,639	43,996	38,354	88,386	79,098	1,135,072	516	1.24
4 1	3 8	1 7 8	182,783	152,925	154,520	143,468	24,512	23,259	49,164	47,711	778,342	427	1.50
1 1	14 7	2 1 1	273,368	229,145	269,663	241,198	15,475	14,047	47,369	44,300	1,134,565	527	1.21
1 0	1 6	9 1 11 5	983,910	787,664	969,059	837,786	181,600	160,100	316,431	285,615	4,522,165	453	1.41
3 9	1 9	0 2 3 2	126,819	98,796	128,377	110,802	25,613	22,811	96,425	85,878	695,521	366	1.75
2 5	1 2	8 1 9 6	273,881	228,450	139,417	124,246	95,925	86,842	97,249	92,451	1,138,461	422	1.52
1 5	0 14	6 1 2 11	386,097	321,094	92,372	77,946	40,792	36,678	33,674	30,508	1,019,161	424	1.51
4 2	1 3	6 1 10 9	462,647	398,764	110,757	97,169	75,540	67,921	84,481	80,989	1,378,268	442	1.45
1 9	0 14	6 1 7 8	380,372	317,803	85,589	74,768	27,434	25,099	36,354	38,677	986,096	427	1.50
3 0	1 2	0 1 9 0	1,629,816	1,364,907	556,512	484,931	265,304	239,351	348,183	328,503	5,217,507	419	1.52
9 9	2 0	4 2 4 2	274,285	231,893	152,452	134,329	14,004	11,909	23,226	20,811	862,909	535	1.20
6 6	2 3	7 2 2 9	315,239	256,987	177,098	146,714	13,551	11,521	42,583	38,318	1,001,961	537	1.19
5 8	1 7	0 1 12 6	389,191	306,376	130,824	110,356	24,861	20,747	41,013	41,239	1,064,607	501	1.28
15 8	1 9	3 1 13 6	347,819	271,840	89,684	71,738	10,637	9,456	16,738	14,802	832,714	412	1.55
3 0	2 0	11 2 4 6	225,376	175,991	96,249	80,542	4,843	4,484	12,166	11,314	610,965	364	1.76
3 1	12 4	2 0 11	1,551,910	1,243,087	646,307	543,679	67,896	58,117	135,676	126,484	4,373,156	465	1.36
6 10	2 4	1 2 10 10	361,396	316,720	213,925	193,091	10,158	9,732	36,614	32,920	1,174,556	500	1.28
6 6	2 3	7 2 12 9	195,857	168,302	127,106	121,172	14,435	13,571	19,904	19,440	679,787	428	1.49
4 3	1 2	10 1 10 7	205,018	175,086	67,863	60,618	7,595	7,084	13,102	12,238	548,604	245	2.61
3 3	1 2	1 1 14 1	258,153	232,162	105,835	97,541	11,872	11,175	14,298	12,836	743,872	247	2.59
3 2	1 12	1 2 3 3	421,873	375,459	208,282	194,313	33,454	31,857	59,189	55,361	1,379,788	495	1.52
1 11	1 9	11 2 3 3	1,442,297	1,267,729	723,011	666,735	77,514	73,419	143,107	132,795	4,526,607	378	1.69
7 3	0 9	9 0 15 3	1,184,954	1,082,559	236,681	212,581	136,121	126,012	57,234	51,732	3,087,874	421	1.52
4 10	1 7	6 1 13 10	646,984	552,355	120,288	107,302	54,922	50,781	62,940	57,678	1,653,251	657	.97
4 12	1 15	9 2 3 0	442,429	378,734	108,690	101,735	22,356	20,992	34,732	34,081	1,143,749	737	.87
4 1	0 2	6 2 1 5	336,134	312,986	193,985	186,793	7,906	7,458	30,724	28,329	1,104,315	214	2.98
6 8	1 15	9 2 2 5	220,243	197,909	181,768	169,196	4,515	4,512	38,252	35,362	851,757	856	.75
1 2	1 6	4 1 9 11	516,592	467,738	231,525	222,229	17,527	17,523	63,128	60,061	1,596,324	732	.87
0 3	1 0	9 1 6 9	3,347,337	2,992,282	1,072,937	999,836	243,347	227,278	287,010	267,243	9,437,270	478	1.34
4 1 1	4 1	1 8 2	9,549,192	8,149,968	4,254,453	3,770,498	996,950	897,320	1,379,941	1,273,560	30,271,885	420	1.52

APPENDIX B.*

From C. Raikes, Esq., Commissioner of Lahore, and Officiating Judge in the Courts of Sudder Dewy. and Nizt. Adawlut, North-west Provinces, Agra.

To H. Ricketts, Esq., Commissioner for the Revision of Civil Salaries and Establishment throughout India.

Dated Agra: the 4th October 1856.

SIR,

I have the honour now to reply to your letter of the 30th April, and to give you my opinion on the several subjects mentioned by you. I have already informed you that as in my present office I have no time to spare from my daily duties, when the Civil Courts are open, I have been compelled to defer my reply to the present time of vacation.

2nd. Before answering *seriatim* the several questions proposed by you, and, indeed, to enable me to answer them at all in an intelligible manner, I must explain my sentiments on the form of Indian government in general.

3rd. There are two systems of government on this side of India, which may shortly be called Regulation and Non-Regulation Systems.

4th. I have served in what are called the Regulation Provinces from 1831 to 1853, and from the beginning of 1853 to the beginning of 1856, in the Non-Regulation Province of the Punjab. Lately I have again been at-

* See p. 171.

N 3

tached to the North-Western Provinces, and in a post which has enabled me to observe the general working of the system of government, and especially in the departments of Civil and Criminal Justice.

5th. In speaking of the two systems, I shall call one the Punjab, and the other the Regulation System.

6th. It would be tedious, and is unnecessary, for me here to trace the various steps which have led to the development of the government of the North-West Provinces in its existing form. But for the sake of contrast with the Punjab System, I must briefly describe the component parts of the administration in these provinces.

7th. In the North-Western Provinces there are thirty-one districts, containing a population, in round numbers, of thirty millions.

To control and administer Civil and Criminal Justice, and to collect the public Revenue in these thirty-one districts, there are six commissioners, each receiving salaries of 38,000 rupees per annum; 19 civil and sessions judges, receiving salaries of 30,000 rupees per annum each; one additional judge at 24,000 rupees per annum; and 31 civil officers holding the joint appointment of magistrate and collector on salaries of 27,000 rupees per annum. Under the magistrates and collectors are 22 joint magistrates with salaries of 12,000 rupees per annum. 10 of the same grade at 8400 rupees per annum, and (say) 40 junior assistants with average salaries of 4800 rupees per annum.

8th. Thus we have for the district local, civil administration in the North-Western Provinces (without taking into account the institutions of Government, Finance, Audit, the high Courts of Appeal, and the Revenue Board at the seat of Government), the following machinery: —

		Rupees.
6 Commissioners of Revenue and Police at	- - -	228,000
19 Civil and Session Judges at	-	570,000
1 additional Judge at	- -	24,000
30 Magistrates and Collectors at	-	810,000
2 Independent Joint Magistrates at -		24,000
20 Joint Magistrates at	- -	240,000
10 Do. do.	- -	84,000
40 Junior Assistants	- -	192,000
Total -	-	2,172,000

These appointments are held by the regularly appointed civil servants of the East India Company.

9th. The agency subordinate to Judges and Magistrates and collectors, exercising judicial functions, or acting as deputies to the collectors of districts are next shown.

Uncovenanted Deputy Collectors.

		Rupees per annum.
2 at 600 per mensem	- -	14,400
20 „ 450 „	- -	108,000
8 „ 350 „	- -	33,600
15 „ 250 „	- -	45,000
Total -	-	201,000

Uncovenanted Judges.

		Rupees per annum.
6 Principal Sudder Ameers at		43,200
14 do. do. do.		67,200
14 Sudder Ameers at	- -	42,000
24 Moonseiffs at	- -	43,200
74 „	- -	88,800
		284,400
Add for Uncovenanted Deputy Collectors -		201,000
Total -	-	485,400

10th. We thus have a staff of Covenanted

	Rupees per ann.
Civil Servants, costing -	- 2,172,000
Civil Servants, not Covenanted -	- 485,400
Total -	- 2,657,400

11th. In considering the administration of the North-Western Provinces, I will refer first to the Civil and Criminal jurisdiction, and then briefly to the Revenue management.

12th. Our judicial system was imported from Bengal, and rests virtually upon the code of 1793. For the regulations enacted in the beginning of the present century, for the ceded and conquered provinces, are mostly copies from those which had been promulgated at an earlier date in Bengal and Benares.

13th. It is important to bear in mind the fact that the system which wise and able men founded in one country, and in one state of society, has been introduced, with few if any modifications, into another country, and into a different state of society. For I may safely assert that the social and physical condition of the North-Western Provinces in 1856, differs very widely from what was the social and physical condition of Bengal in 1793.

14th. In Bengal sixty years ago, it was rightly considered safer and better to rely upon institutions rather than upon men. Hence, to use the words of an able modern writer, we have a judicial "system which does not depend for its success upon extraordinary individual efforts, but which is susceptible of effective superintendence and development." (Preface to Macpherson's Procedure of the Civil Courts of the East India Company.)

15th. To carry out this "strictly organised and regulated" system, we have an apparatus of highly-paid Judges, whose powers are limited to the administration of civil justice, the trial of criminal cases at the Sessions, and the hearing of appeals from orders passed by the magistrates in criminal trials.

16th. Under them again are (more or less) 125 native or other uncovenanted judges, the bulk of whom receive a very scanty salary, and who decide civil suits, giving occasional aid to the magistrate in cases of small importance in the criminal department.

17th. The salary of the judge is not much more than that of the magistrate and collector; his duties are of a description less interesting, less stirring, and on the whole more irksome. Though the judge is the superior officer in the district, the magistrate is the more important and influential personage. The magistrate is to the people the direct and powerful representative of the Government, has large patronage, and a wide discretion and power, which the judge may fetter or restrain, but cannot exercise in his own person.

18th. The result of this is, that where the judge, and the collector, and magistrate are both earnest and zealous men, there is a probability of a conflict of opinion, and a possibility of great soreness and discontent on the part of the magistrate when the judge reverses his orders.

19th. To glance hastily at the Revenue system. Here we find that the orders of the highly educated European magistrate and collector in Revenue cases, concerning rent, replevin, or ouster are liable to be revised and reversed in a regular suit before a half-educated native moonsiff, on a salary of 100 rupees per mensem. (The natives are never tired of wondering at anomalies of this sort.)

20th. Again, the magistrate and collector in Police and Revenue matters is subordinate to the Commissioner. Whatever may be the cause, the effect of the relative position of the two officers as at present regulated is not always harmony and order, and in a word, what it ought to be, subordination. It has been the generous custom of the senior members of the Civil Service to encourage freedom of opinion and discussion amongst the juniors; but this has been carried too far in many instances, and owing to this, and to the divided authority under which they labour, the magistrates and collectors, especially the more earnest men, have sometimes allowed themselves to forget the respect due to their official superiors. That such feelings have not formed the rule instead of the exception, is due to the good feeling and high principle so general in the service.

21st. I feel quite sure that the divided and remote nature of the control exercised by the judge and by the commissioner has a tendency to provoke opposition; and as the native ministerial officers and suitors, with a weakness common to their race, delight in fomenting quarrels, and in widening those breaches of courtesy which may unfortunately find place in official communications, no efforts on their part are wanting if they fancy there is an opportunity for creating or for increasing discussion.

22nd. The result of all this is, that our system of district administration, though in many respects efficient, can hardly be said to work well. There is too much friction in the component parts of the machinery, and too little unity of action. The evil-disposed intriguing part of the native population take advantage of this to set one officer or one system against another. If they cannot prosecute an enemy successfully in the criminal department, they try to harass him in the Civil Courts; if they find a magistrate or collector too active and vigorous, they endeavour to set the judge or the commissioner in opposition to him.

23rd. The idea, so natural to the European mind, that it would be unjust or impolitic for one and the same man to act as District Chief in matters of Revenue, Police, and Civil Justice, never entered into the mind of a native in India. They laugh at the division and consequent frittering away of power in the Regulation Provinces, and take advantage of the liberal and noble spirit of the Government to impede and restrict the free course of truth and justice.

24th. In a word, the natives of India are not fit, and will not be fit, to judge from the past, for centuries to come, for a Government carried on upon these principles, which suit a people who (like their rulers the British) are capable of self-government.

25th. To give them a Government on those principles is to *retard their progress,* to set the mass of the people against the ruling power, and to benefit sycophants and rogues.

26th. Social progress under the simpler *quasi* Oriental system is far more rapid than under the artificial system of checks which is established in the Regulation Provinces. I boldly assert that in the Jullunder Daob, the Lahore and Jhelum Divisions, and doubtless other parts of the Punjab, a greater progress has been made in five years than has been made in any of the Regulation Provinces in fifty. I know this to be a fact; and a reference to the Criminal Statistics of those Divisions will prove the truth of my assertion.

27th. The people there find themselves under a District Chief who has all legitimate power in his hands. Should he abuse or exceed that power, they have the Commissioner to look to for redress. The public interests of the Commissioner and of the Deputy Commissioner being identical, and the Deputy being unable (if he wished so to do) to resist the will and authority of his principal, the work goes on smoothly, harmoniously, and well. If it does not so go on, it is not the fault of the system, at all events; and my own experience is, that a Deputy Commissioner and Commissioner work together LIKE ONE MAN.

28th. My experience, on the other hand, in the Regulation Provinces is, that when an energetic, earnest Magistrate and Collector works in perfect harmony with his

Judge and Commissioner, it is owing to unusual temper
and tact on the part of the subordinate, or extreme for-
bearance on the part of the superior officer.

29th. I therefore consider that, for India, the system
introduced by our late Governor-General in the Punjab
is the best.

30th. But both Commissioners and Deputy Commissioners in the Punjab are overworked and under-paid;
and I therefore give below the scale of pay and the number
and designation of officers which I would suggest for the
North-Western Provinces,—so far as the District work is
concerned.

PROPOSED SCALE OF OFFICERS AND SALARIES FOR
THE NORTH-WESTERN PROVINCES, ON THE PUNJAB
PLAN, MODIFIED AND IMPROVED.

Covenanted Officers.

No.	Office.	Salaries of each, per mensem.	Salaries of all, per annum.
		Rupees.	Rupees.
15	Commissioners - - -	3000	540,000
30	Deputy Commissioners - -	2000	720,000
10	Assistants, 1st grade - -	1000	120,000
20	Ditto, 2nd ditto - -	700	168,000
40	Ditto, 3rd ditto - -	400	192,000
115			1,740,000

Then for Uncovenanted Assistants.

No.	Office.	Salaries of each, per mensem.	Salaries of all, per annum.
		Rupees.	Rupees.
10	Extra Uncovenanted Assistants	600	72,000
20	Ditto - - - - -	400	96,000
90	Ditto - - - - -	200	216,000
120			384,000

Total Expense of District Administration in the North-West Provinces.

	Rupees.
As at present - - - - - -	2,657,000
Proposed on Punjab System - - -	2,124,000
Annual Saving by Punjab System - - -	Rs. 53,300

Thus each District would have a Deputy Commissioner with two Assistants, with one Extra Assistant at 600 rs. or 400 rs. per mensem, and three Extra Assistants at 200 rs. per mensem. With this Staff, and with Tehseeldars exercising Judicial and Criminal, as well as Revenue, powers,— the Deputy Commissioner trying, in general, Appeals only (in Civil suits), and educating his first Assistant as a Judge, by giving him the heavy Judicial cases; with one Commissioner over two Deputies, who could not only support these Deputies, but also keep them in perfect order,— the work would be done with *complete despatch and efficiency,* and at a considerable saving.

31st. If the districts were thus managed and the Punjab Arms Act introduced, as it ought to be, across the length and breadth of the land, as well as a simple code of civil procedure, and a modification of the existing criminal law, there would be more order, prosperity, and internal tranquillity in Hindoostan than in any part of the world. At present we are in advance of many European countries and but little behind England in these respects. With the alterations I have sketched we should soon be un-rivalled in the world. For the Indian races are amongst the most industrious, commercial, orderly, and contented people in the world, if only kept in order.

32nd. The Asiatic system of a mild despotism suits them, and it is only under a system of paternal or despotic restraint that they will ever become capable of self-improvement and consequently fit for self-government.

33rd. Intelligent, honourable, and industrious English-

men, guided, controlled, or stimulated by the able hands
of such men as have been always selected for the post of
Lieutenant-Governor or Chief Commissioner in the Upper
Provinces will, when free to act as in the Punjab, accomplish wonders and bring unexampled social order and commercial prosperity over the land.

34th. Such men will not waste their lives, abilities, and
prospects in India on niggardly salaries such as may suffice
for the judge of a county court or a stipendiary magistrate
in England. Superior men will not accept inferior emolu-
ments, and we want superior men for this work. A few
able men well paid will do more for India than a larger
staff of average mediocrity.

35th. The distant threats of cutting down salaries have
already, I observe, taken effect; and it is notorious in
England that a petty living of 200*l.* or 300*l.* per annum
already holds out greater inducements to men of learning
and talent than the Civil Service of India. The candi-
dates for examination this year are far too few and only
half in number of those of last year, although this year we
have peace and last year were plunged in war.

36th. I need not allude to the higher offices of state
held by the members of the Sudder Court and Board of
Revenue at Agra, as some such machinery of government
must be kept up and at the present expense. But with
reference to the proposed constitution of the High Court
will only express my conviction that it is a mistake, and a
very dangerous one, to place natives into appointments
where they will have to control European officers.

37th. I would ask whether is more of moral courage,
self-reliance, candour, and intellectual light required in
the office of a chief-justice or of a general of division?

38th. When natives are found fit to command our
armies, brigades, or even regiments, it will be time to
place them on the bench of the High Courts.

39th. They have as much physical courage as their

English rulers, are as well fitted for soldiers, but are not fit to command their own countrymen, still less are they qualified by nature or habit to command Englishmen.

40th. If then it be true, as who will doubt, that natives are unfit to command our armies, so are they equally unfitted to rule over councils, or as judges in the courts of appeal to exercise supreme control over our judicial and magisterial officers. Why should an English judge be placed under a Mahometan or Brahmin judge any more than an English colonel be put under a Brahmin general?

41st. Having ventured at some length to place before you my opinion as to the most really economical and effectual mode of district administration in these provinces I proceed to answer the queries proposed in your letter, which after the full explanation of my sentiments here given may be very briefly recorded.

42nd. *First Question.*—Would it be advantageous to introduce grades of salaries in the judicial and revenue departments? How many grades of magistrates, of collectors, of judges, and of commissioners would you have?

Answer.—I have fully answered this question in paragraphs 30 to 31, but I may add here that I think that every district chief should get a salary of 24,000 rupees per annum. If grades are introduced as a matter of economy so much the worse for the country, in my opinion. It is inconvenient to the local government to attach certain salaries to certain very large or difficult districts, because every district has its own peculiar difficulties, and the man who may be invaluable in one comparatively easy district from his local knowledge, may merit as high a salary as another officer who is selected for the charge of a very large and important district. I advocate one rate of salary of 2000 rupees per mensem for every magistrate and collector, deputy-commissioner.

43rd. *Second Question.*—Could we advantageously make further use of native agency by increasing the powers of deputy-collectors, deputy-magistrates, monlovees, pundits, moonsiffs, and tehseelders?

Answer. — Collectors can at present make over most cases, however difficult or important, to be decided by their Native Deputies. I would not increase the powers of native subordinates, as they have now, when authorised by Government, as much power as the covenanted European Deputy Collector or Joint Magistrate.

44th. *Third Question.* — Would it be advantageous to separate the Police altogether from the Magistracy and to have a Superintendent of Police in each District?

Answer. — I think it would be a step in the wrong direction to separate the Police and the Magistracy. All power in India, to suit the genius and wants of the people and their simple state of civilisation, should be placed in the same hand. The degrees of power only, and not the nature of power, should be strictly limited and defined. This is the secret of successful government in Asia.

45th. *Fourth Question.* — Would it be advisable to increase the powers of magistrates and to give them authority to pass sentence of Seven or Ten Years' Imprisonment, their notes in English, with an abstract of the case, to be forwarded for the information of the Session Judge when the sentence may exceed three years?

Answer. — If the District Chief receive a salary of 24,000 rupees, it is reasonable to suppose that he will be an officer of 10 years' standing. In that case I think it would be an improvement to increase the powers of the Magistrate in the manner here proposed.

46th. *Fifth Question.* — Does your experience tell you that to give a Session's Judge the power to set aside a Magistrate's order is productive of much mischief, and that it would be beneficial to rule that a second opinion should be taken before an order is reversed? If you think a second opinion should be taken, by what measures could a reference be most conveniently provided?

Answer.—I have already, in Paragraphs 17 to 30, shown what I consider the best remedy for the clashing between Judge and Magistrate, and Magistrate and Commissioner. The way to correct this is to give the Judge or Commissioner an identical interest, differing only in *degree* with that of the District Chief. I think that it would be better for Judges to reverse Magistrates' orders as they do now than to complicate the machinery of Government further by requiring a second opinion before a Judge could reverse. If, however, a referee be required the Commissioner should be the man. But I could never recommend so cumbersome a check.

47th. *Sixth Question.*—Could the quantity of business now carried to the Sudder Courts be advantageously diminished by the Establishment of District or Divisional Courts with a European and two Native Judges sitting together for the disposal of certain classes of cases now carried to the Sudder Courts?

Answer. — In taking up appeals from Sudder Ameers or Moonsiffs, I should not object to see two Native Judges employed instead of one. Differences of opinion to be submitted for the orders of the District Judge, whose decision would be final. I should not wish to see a European Judge and two Native Judges on the same bench.

48th. *Seventh Question.* — How could the position of Sale Ameers under regulation 1 of 1839, be improved? Should other agency for the sale of distrained property be provided, or should the power of distraint be altogether withdrawn? Would it be well to transfer the trial of summary suits to Moonsiffs, or to station Deputy Collectors in the Mofussil, with powers to try them?

Answer. — My experience only enables me to suggest, with reference to the last of these queries, that in the North-West Provinces I think it very desirable that the local government should have and exercise the power of investing the Tehseeldars with powers to try summary suits,

O

subject to appeal to the Collector, who might make such appeals over to his Deputies, covenanted or uncovenanted. I adopted this plan in the Punjab and found it answer very well. In Bengal, where the services of Tehseeldars are not available, I presume it would be a good plan to make summary suits over to the Moonsiffs.

49th. *Eighth Question.* — Might it not be advantageous to increase the powers of Collectors and Commissioners, and to allow no appeals in cases which can be carried into the Civil Courts?

Answer. — The best plan, in my humble opinion, is that which I have sketched in Paragraphs 17 to 30 of this letter. But as it is not very probable that my suggestions will be adopted, I certainly think that it would be an improvement on the existing system if all suits for land and rent were decided entirely by the Collector and Commissioner, and were no longer preferred in the Civil Courts. This would put the agricultural interest, as such, under one set of masters.

50th. In conclusion, I beg to apologise for my own opinions thus hastily put together, by one more remark.

51st. There are, as I have remarked, two systems for Indian Government strangely growing up side by side, and each receiving daily fresh development.

The one, the *legal* or Regulation System, just in theory but unsuited in practice to the wants and genius of Asiatics. This is the system which finds favour with English lawyers, who guide the public mind of England in such questions. And this system, itself faulty, is being patched and perverted by certain pseudo-philanthropists at home who fondly believe that an English gentleman, when once landed in India, forgets the habits, instincts, and religion of his forefathers, and becomes an advocate for injustice, torture, and tyranny. These gentlemen philanthropists over-estimate the native capacity for Civil Government and for Self-Government in proportion as they undervalue the integrity, ability, and public spirit of their fellow-countrymen in India.

53rd. The other system, combining the Oriental plan, and therefore so far suiting the people, with the virtues of Christianity and so far protecting them, is the Punjab system as introduced by the Marquis of Dalhousie. The object of this scheme of government is to combine all the avowed excellencies of the Revenue System of the North-West provinces, with a sure and simple form of Civil and Criminal Justice.

54th. Officers are as far as possible well selected, well supervised, and freely trusted. They ought to be also better paid than is now the case.

55th. Under Lord Dalhousie's Government and the mixed system of English and Oriental Government, many parts of the Punjab have progressed from anarchy to civilisation at a rate which is incredible to those who have not, as I have, witnessed and examined the marvellous change.

I have the honour to be, Sir,

Your most obedient servant,

(Signed) CHARLES RAIKES.

Commr. and Supt. of Lahore, and Offig. Judge of the Sudr. Dy. and Neizt. Adwt. N. W. P. Agra.

Agra: the 4th of October, 1856.

THE END.

LONDON
PRINTED BY SPOTTISWOODE AND CO.
NEW-STREET SQUARE

* 9 7 8 1 8 4 7 3 4 2 7 6 8 *